"Barry and Emily McCarthy have authored a number of outstanding texts concerning human sexuality for the general public. Their latest book, *Couple Sexuality After 60*, offers a compassionate understanding of sexuality in aging couples. It offers sophisticated yet practical advice. I encourage anyone over 60 to purchase, enjoy, and contemplate the wisdom offered by this internationally respected clinician."

Robert Taylor Segraves, MD, PhD, *Professor of Psychiatry, Case Western Reserve University, Editor,* Journal of Sex and Marital Therapy

"Barry and Emily McCarthy have created yet another masterpiece! Skillfully guiding readers through the nuances of maintaining a satisfying sex life well into old age, the McCarthys steer professional and lay audiences alike through the myriad of misinformation, misunderstanding, and fallacies that haunt our views of sex and aging. Their writing style is clear and inviting. Their suggested exercises are thoughtful and practical. And their optimism regarding sex and aging is refreshing, wise, and sound. I know I will recommend this book to my aging patients, those with and without partners."

Daniel N. Watter, EdD, *Past President, Society for Sex Therapy and Research (SSTAR)*

"This self-help book for seniors is the culmination of the authors' highly productive writing partnership. A long married couple, the McCarthys provide guidance that revolves around two models: Good Enough Sex and Female–Male Sexual Equity. These well explained themes and their variations are delivered in a conversational style inspiring readers to rethink their previous sexual patterns, accept their regrets over past errors, and get right to a better, variable, sensual, pleasurable life, with or without intercourse. Their messages are wise: do not give up on sexual behavior and keep discovering your capacities!"

Stephen B. Levine, MD, *author of* Psychotherapeutic Approaches to Sexual Problems: An Essential Guide for Mental Health Professionals

"*Couple Sexuality After 60* will surprise and enlighten readers of any age, but will prove most valuable to men and women hoping to enhance their sexual experience as they grow older. The McCarthys disprove many of the myths surrounding sex and aging. Even better, they offer their readers new perspectives, dismissing performance-oriented sex and embracing a realistic positive attitude towards couple sexuality in which 'intimate and erotic allies turn to each other and share pleasure.' Their focus on responsive desire, more genuine and human than the spontaneous desire associated with youth, is a highlight of the book."

Katharine Bethell, MSW, *author of* An Essential Guide to Aging Well

"If you are 60 or older, and mourning the loss of youthful and effortless sex, take heart. What you will find in the pages of this book may upend all you have ever believed about sex. But then sex after 60 is different than the sex that came before, in ways that may be as unexpected as they are pleasurable. Written for couples to read together, this book promises to help older couples become intimate and erotic allies who turn towards each other to embrace a new and pleasurable sexuality."

Kathryn Hall, PhD, *Editor,* Principles and Practice of Sex Therapy, *6th edition, Past President, Society for Sex Therapy and Research (SSTAR)*

"With Barry and Emily McCarthy's 16th book, *Couple Sexuality After 60*, arrives added consensus that the sexuality writing team constitute a blooming 'national treasure.' Their immense gift to the nation is highlighted by their work's contrast with the dismal sexual culture it addresses.

The authors offer new perspectives on sexual cultural deficits in the US like double standards, ageism, abstinence-only sex education, LGBTQIA+phobia, high STI and sexual violence rates, sexual performance anxiety, reproductive injustice, devaluation of the erotic, and more. They also describe how to love well despite personally damaging national attitudes and policies.

The new book's insightful myth-bashing, concepts like 'good enough sex' and finding a sexual style, and helpful guidance on fostering desire and on appreciating differences, aims to shift attitudes and open hearts to greater mutuality and satisfaction.

If Barry and Emily's *Couple Sexuality After 60* were the only resource teens had for sex education, they would be well prepared for satisfying sexuality throughout their lives. Although this book probably won't be marketed to teens, it will serve its intended audience well.

Baby boomers will spark to its directness and honesty, plain speaking usefulness, cutting edge knowledge, excellent selection of topics, no-nonsense elevation of sex as entitlement, peak experience, and relationship sustenance. They will love the inspiration to keep sexuality the important part of their lives it has always been for this generation.

A wise book and fun read for professionals and common readers alike."

Susan Stiritz, *Immediate Past President of AASECT, Associate Professor of Practice, Chair, Specialization in Sexual Health and Education, The Brown School, Washington University, St. Louis*

COUPLE SEXUALITY AFTER 60

Confronting taboos and misunderstandings about sexuality and aging, *Couple Sexuality After 60: Intimate, Pleasurable, and Satisfying* motivates couples to embrace sex and sexuality in their 60s, 70s, and 80s. The book busts two extreme myths—that people over 60 cannot and should not be sexual and that the best way to be sexual is to emphasize eroticism, using sex toys, and "kinky sex".

Using a variable, flexible approach to couple sexuality based on the Good Enough Sex (GES) model, this book places the essence of sexuality in pleasure-oriented touching, not individual sex performance. Barry and Emily McCarthy introduce a new sexual mantra of "desire/pleasure/eroticism/satisfaction" with the goal of presenting a healthy model of sexuality to replace the traditional double standard that couples learn in young adulthood. Specific chapters focus on important areas like coming to terms with the new normal, female–male sexual equity, satisfaction being about more than intercourse and orgasm, valuing synchronous and asynchronous sexuality, psychobiosocial approaches to sexuality, and more.

In addition to aging heterosexual couples, single individuals and queer couples will find this book interesting. Additionally, sexual health clinicians and sex therapists with clients over the age of 60 will find this a fascinating read.

Barry McCarthy is professor emeritus of psychology at American University, a diplomate in clinical psychology, a diplomate in sex therapy, and a certified couple therapist. He is the author of over 100 articles, 33 book chapters, and 21 books. He has presented over 450 professional workshops nationally and internationally. Barry received the Society for Sex Therapy and Research (SSTAR) Masters and Johnson award for lifetime contributions to the sex therapy field.

Emily McCarthy received a BS degree in speech communication, and her writing and wisdom provide a balanced humanistic perspective. This is Barry and Emily's 16th co-authored book.

COUPLE SEXUALITY AFTER 60

Intimate, Pleasurable, and Satisfying

Barry McCarthy and Emily McCarthy

Routledge
Taylor & Francis Group
NEW YORK AND LONDON

First published 2022
by Routledge
605 Third Avenue, New York, NY 10158

and by Routledge
2 Park Square, Milton Park, Abingdon, Oxon OX14 4RN

Routledge is an imprint of the Taylor & Francis Group, an informa business

Library of Congress Cataloging-in-Publication Data
A catalog record for this title has been requested

ISBN: 9780367491703 (hbk)
ISBN: 9780367491710 (pbk)
ISBN: 9781003044888 (ebk)

Typeset in Perpetua
by Newgen Publishing UK

CONTENTS

1

CONFRONTING MYTHS ABOUT SEXUALITY AND AGING

Aging and sexuality are two socially taboo topics surrounded by myths and silence. People believe "common sense" ideas even when they have no scientific support or there is evidence that they are false. How much do you really know about sexuality and aging? We ask you to take the following true/false test—don't worry about performance anxiety, your answers will not be graded.

1. Few couples have intercourse after age 60.
2. Women are glad when their husbands agree to stop sex.
3. Menopause destroys female desire and orgasmic response.
4. The choice to stop sex is usually mutual.
5. Viagra or Cialis ensure reliable erections into your 70s.
6. Adult children urge their parents to stay sexually active.
7. The more educated the couple, the easier to accept the cessation of sex.
8. When couples stop intercourse they increase manual and oral sex as a substitute.
9. Sexual satisfaction dramatically decreases after age 60.
10. Intercourse is a necessary activity to prove sexual desire.
11. The key for male desire is a spontaneous erection.
12. Gay men stop being sexual because they can't have an erection sufficient for anal intercourse.
13. Lesbian women are affectionate, not sexual, after age 60.

14. Rates of sexual crimes, especially voyeurism, increase with aging.
15. Aging men are more likely to sexually abuse children than are adolescent or young adult men.
16. Porn use increases after age 70.
17. With decreased lubrication, painful intercourse occurs with almost all women after age 60.
18. Viagra, Cialis, or penile injections are the best way to ensure predictable erections with aging.
19. "Responsive sexual desire" only applies to women, not men.
20. Grandparents are very judgmental about the sexuality of their adult children and grandchildren.
21. Religious older couples have less sex than non-religious couples.
22. Older single men have lots of sex partners, but older single women have few sexual options.
23. Masturbation is a sign of poor mental health.
24. Using erotic fantasies or materials indicates sexual compulsivity.
25. Sex is not important for older couples.

Count the number of trues you listed. This was a sex and aging myth test. All items are false.

Old myths are based on sexual ignorance and repressive beliefs. New myths are based on sex performance demands and erotic perfectionism. Myths die hard—they have a life of their own. Myths are difficult to confront and change. Knowledge is power. This is particularly true regarding sexuality and aging.

We have been looking forward to writing this book for years. We are enthusiastic about sharing the good news—not only can you continue to be sexual in your 60s, 70s, and 80s, but enjoying pleasure-oriented sexuality is good for your psychological, physical, and relational well-being (McCarthy & McCarthy, 2019). The role of sexuality is to energize your bond and reinforce feelings of desire and desirability. Sexuality has a small, integral 15–20% role in individual and couple well-being. Enjoying pleasure and sexuality enhances your life and relationship. Sadly, when you stop being sexual it has an inordinately powerful negative impact, draining intimacy and demoralizing you.

Contrary to "common sense" beliefs, when aging couples stop being sexual it is almost always the man's choice because he has lost confidence with erections and intercourse (Lindau et al., 2007). He says to himself, "I don't want to start something I can't finish". This is a unilateral choice which is conveyed non-verbally. Being non-sexual is a loss for the man, woman, and couple. This is true even for women and couples who experience low desire and sex dysfunction. You not only stop intercourse, but also stop sensual, playful, and erotic touching. Sadly, many couples also cease affectionate touch. The paradox is that sex dysfunction, conflict, and avoidance have a more negative impact than the role of healthy sexuality. This is particularly true for men. Stopping sexual expression is harmful for your psychological and physical well-being. You become the stereotypical "grumpy old man" who is negative about a range of topics including relationships and sexuality. Men who stop being sexual are prone to depression and alcohol abuse. You become isolated, frustrated, and alienated.

In examining sex myths, it is important to not only confront these mistaken beliefs, but to establish scientifically validated information which is personally relevant and promotes psychological, relational, and sexual well-being. Let us explore each myth and examine healthy understandings. Remember, respect individual, couple, cultural, and value differences. Sexually, one size never fits all. Sexual knowledge promotes well-being.

1. The good news is that the majority of couples are sexual at age 60, including enjoying intercourse. The bad news is that about one in three couples stop being sexual by age 65 and two in three by age 75. You can be sexual in your 60s, 70s, and 80s, but it means transitioning to a variable, flexible couple sexuality rather than defining sex as an individual pass–fail intercourse performance test. A key is defining sexuality to include sensual, playful, and erotic scenarios in addition to intercourse. The empowering strategy for couple sexuality with aging is to adopt the GES model (Metz & McCarthy, 2012). The core of sexuality is giving and receiving pleasure-oriented touching and developing positive, realistic sexual expectations. About 85% of sexual encounters will flow to intercourse. When it doesn't flow,

rather than panicking or apologizing, transition to an erotic or sensual scenario. GES has a range of roles, meanings, and outcomes that promote variable, flexible couple sexuality.

2. It is men who choose to end sex because you have lost confidence with erections and intercourse. You do this unilaterally and convey it non-verbally. This is a self-defeating choice for the man, woman, and couple. Not only do you stop intercourse, but also sensual, playful, and erotic touching. Ceasing sexuality is demoralizing for you and robs your relationship of intimacy and vitality. The "wise" decision is to be aware that sexuality involves sensual, playful, and erotic scenarios in addition to intercourse. Turn toward each other as intimate and erotic friends, do not turn away and avoid the spouse when sex is not functional. Embrace GES, focus on sharing pleasure, and accept variable, flexible sexuality. Women, including those with low desire, non-orgasmic response, or sexual pain, miss intimacy and touching. Few older couples divorce, but you mourn the loss of physical and emotional attachment.
3. Women experience menopause in their early 50s, although some experience peri-menopause symptoms in their mid-30s and others not until their late 50s. Hormonal and lubrication changes do not stop sexual desire (the core sexual dimension). Attitudes and reactions to menopause illustrate the importance of utilizing the psychobiosocial approach to sexuality. You can enjoy your body more after menopause. A key factor is accepting use of additional vaginal lubrication. Build sexual receptivity and responsivity before transitioning to intercourse. Understanding and accepting your body with aging is crucial. Rather than being fearful or controlled by anti-sex beliefs, a key to menopause is accepting the transition and using all your psychological, biomedical, and relational resources to maintain sexual integrity (Ghazzani, 2020). A strategy many women use is to initiate and guide intromission at high levels of subjective arousal. Utilize intercourse positions and types of thrusting which facilitate arousal rather than the traditional man-on-top position with short, rapid thrusting. Feel accepted as a sexual woman before, during, and after menopause.

4. The "politically correct" belief is that stopping sex is mutual. However, in over 90% of cases the choice to stop is the man's. This shocks both the public and professionals. It is the opposite of the male–female double standard. The man doesn't want to stop sex. You stop because you have lost confidence with erections and intercourse. You can't live up to the demands of perfect sex performance. You are trapped in the cycle of anticipatory anxiety, performance anxiety, frustration, embarrassment, and eventually sexual avoidance. You believe the myth that intercourse is the only acceptable type of sex. You say to yourself, "I don't want to start something I can't finish". You blame the woman which is particularly unfair and alienating. The solution is to have a genuine dialogue which confronts the "intercourse or nothing" model. Embracing GES with a focus on sharing pleasure is the healthiest strategy. Especially important is enjoying sensual and erotic scenarios. Do not panic or apologize. Whether the erotic scenario is mutual and synchronous or asynchronous (positive, but better for one partner than the other), it allows you to end the experience in a positive manner.
5. You hope that a stand-alone medical intervention will deliver the results shown on tv ads—totally predictable erections. Viagra or Cialis can be a resource in rebuilding sexual confidence. What pro-erection medications cannot do is be a stand-alone intervention which returns you to the easy, predictable erections of your 20s. You feel you are the only man who has failed with Viagra. In truth, almost all men fail to get 100% predictable erections. The most important factor is to turn toward the partner as your intimate and erotic ally rather than expect the medication to do it all. Even among men who respond well to Viagra or Cialis, very few achieve 100% reliable erections. Be an intimate sexual team, do not expect a medication to do it all (Althof, 2006). Be sexually present. Most important, adopt the GES model which emphasizes variable, flexible couple sexuality and positive, realistic expectations (65–85% of encounters flow to intercourse).
6. Only one in four adult children believe their parents are sexually active and only one in 13 believe their grandparents are still sexual.

It is unlikely that you will receive family support for sexuality and aging. Nor are you likely to receive encouragement from the culture or friends. Adopt a pro-sexual stance and approach your spouse as your intimate and erotic friend. Commit to "beating the odds" and enjoy pleasure-oriented sexuality with aging.

7. The more educated the couple the more likely you will stay sexually involved and feel sexually satisfied. Knowledge is power. The more you understand and accept the psychobiosocial approach to sexuality and aging the better. It's especially important to establish positive, realistic sexual expectations.
8. Intercourse is an integral part of sexuality and aging, but not intercourse as an individual pass–fail performance test. When couples stop intercourse, they usually stop manual and oral sexuality. It becomes "intercourse or nothing" with the result being nothing. GES advocates for sensual, playful, and erotic scenarios as integral to your sexuality. Manual and oral sexuality are healthy expressions of eroticism. Value this for itself, not as a substitute for intercourse. Manual and oral sexuality are more satisfying when subjective arousal is at least a 6 (on a 10-point scale). When arousal is low, using oral sex as a desperate attempt to service your partner feels anti-erotic. Oral and manual sexuality can be synchronous or asynchronous.
9. Sexual satisfaction increases with aging, especially for couples who emphasize sharing pleasure and accept GES. Satisfaction involves feeling good about yourself as a sexual person and feeling energized as a sexual couple. Satisfaction involves orgasm, but is much more than orgasm. A key for satisfaction is acceptance of the sexual experience whether it was wonderful, good, okay, or dysfunctional. Turn toward your partner as your intimate friend. No blaming or apologizing. By its nature, sexuality and aging is variable and flexible with a range of roles, meanings, and outcomes.
10. Desire is not measured by intercourse frequency. The essence of desire is sexual anticipation, sense of deserving pleasure, freedom and choice, and a range of sexual scenarios and techniques. If every sexual experience had to involve high desire ending in intercourse, this demand would eventually subvert your desire. Desire is facilitated

by openness and willingness to engage sexually. Desire is subverted by the demand for goal-oriented intercourse.

11. For adolescent and young adult men the sign of sexual desire is easy, spontaneous erections. The key for men over 60 is "responsive sexual desire". Typically, you begin at neutral (0) arousal. As you engage in giving and receiving affectionate, sensual, and playful touching your subjective arousal is 2–4. You experience subjective arousal first and then feel sexual desire. Your desire promotes your partner's desire and her desire promotes couple desire. Desire is a response to emotional openness and physical pleasure rather than expecting a spontaneous erection or high levels of eroticism.
12. Gay couples are sexual in their 60s, 70s, and 80s. Although anal intercourse remains a favorite form of sexual expression for many gay couples, others switch to manual, oral, or rubbing stimulation. In the past, older gay men felt stigmatized and not desirable or attractive. In gay sexuality, there is a growing recognition of the importance of integrating intimacy, pleasuring, and eroticism. It is crucial to confront the myths and prejudices against older gay sex—many of which, sadly, are shared in the gay community. Self-acceptance is crucial. Take pride in celebrating gay sexuality with aging.
13. The prejudice against older lesbian women is rampant, including in the lesbian community. The challenge with lesbian couples is to integrate eroticism into your couple sexual style. Lesbian couples value desire/pleasure/eroticism/satisfaction in your 60s, 70s, and 80s. Aging lesbian couples enjoy vital and satisfying sexuality.
14. One of the most destructive myths is that older men engage in sex crimes. The reality is the opposite. Most sex crimes are committed by adolescent and young adult men. Very low rates occur in older men. This is also true for cybersex and internet sex—low rates of misuse by older men.
15. Another common myth is that older men are at high risk for sex offenses against children, including their own grandchildren. In reality, rates of child sex abuse are very low for older men. A positive role for older adults (females and males) is to be sex educators and life coaches for your grandchildren. Grandchildren benefit from

grandparents who care about and support their growth and development (including sexually).

16. Masturbation is normal and healthy whether at 77, 47, or 17. This is true for women and men, married or single. Of course, people misuse masturbation, especially as a compulsive secret pattern or a way to avoid partner sex. Aging people masturbate for pleasure and tension reduction which is normal and healthy.
17. Erotic fantasies and porn, which often accompany masturbation, is a complex and controversial topic. The best way to understand porn is as a fantasy dimension. What gives porn its erotic charge is that it is different than what you experience sexually. What works in porn is totally different than real-life couple sexuality. Around 85% of men and 97% of women who use porn do so in a way that does not disrupt the person or relationship. What makes porn problematic is the combination of high secrecy, high eroticism, and high shame—this is a "poison pill".
18. Vaginal lubrication is not a good measure of subjective arousal. Older women usually utilize additional lubrication to facilitate intercourse. Painful intercourse is a problem for a significant number of women. You can utilize a range of strategies to make sex comfortable and enjoyable. In addition to vaginal lubrication this includes mindfulness; your partner being a sexual ally in dealing with pain; enhanced subjective arousal; not transitioning to intercourse until experiencing erotic flow; using slower, longer, or circular thrusting; utilizing multiple stimulation before and during intercourse. You deserve to enjoy aging sexuality, including intercourse.
19. The drug companies tell men and their partners that a stand-alone medical intervention (Viagra, Cialis, or testosterone) will guarantee erections. They sell drugs by lying and overpromising. You can enjoy erections and intercourse in your 60s, 70s, and 80s—that's the good news. The bad news is that you can't have the easy, totally predictable erections you experienced in your 20s. You have "grown-up" erections rather than hoping for "show-up" erections. Accept variable, flexible male and couple sexuality and embrace GES. Perhaps 65–85% of sexual encounters will flow from comfort to pleasure to arousal to

erotic flow to intercourse and orgasm. Intercourse is enhanced by pro-erection medications which help maintain an erection when you are feeling aroused. Penile injections can cause erections, but must be integrated into your couple sexual style of intimacy, pleasuring, and eroticism. Couples stop using injections because it feels mechanical.

20. "Responsive sexual desire" is a breakthrough concept developed with women, but is of great value for aging men. In responsive desire you engage in pleasuring and are mindful of emotional needs which build receptivity and responsivity. You feel desire when subjective arousal is in the 2–4 range on a 10-point scale where 0 is neutral, 5 is beginning sexual arousal, and 10 is orgasm. Pleasure and willingness promote desire. Rather than hoping for spontaneous desire, embrace responsive sexual desire.
21. Grandparents want their adult children and grandchildren to be healthy sexual people. Although there are negative and judgmental grandparents, they are in the minority. They are motivated by fear that sex will interfere with the child's development. Grandparents can provide a healthy model for relationships and sexuality—a valuable resource for adult children and grandchildren.
22. Religious couples, especially religions that emphasize God as a loving, supportive deity, do better sexually than non-religious couples. In 2021, almost all religions are pro-sex in marriage. Typically, religion emphasizes intimacy and security, but ignores the role of eroticism and sexual vitality. Religious communities reinforce satisfying and secure marriages. Unfortunately, most ministers ignore the topic of healthy sexuality. A sermon about the importance of sexuality and aging would be of great value.
23. The male–female double standard is particularly destructive for older single people. The mistaken notion that men have their choice of women (especially younger women) and enjoy casual sex is intimidating, not motivating. Few older men thrive with these performance demands. The cultural stereotype of the lonely, non-sexual older woman is demoralizing and stigmatizing. You are capable of enjoying both self and partner sexual expression. You are a sexual person throughout your life.

24. Myths about masturbation negatively impact men and women, married and single. There are few resources which provide information on the psychological and physical benefits of masturbation. Not only is masturbation not a symptom of poor mental health, it is a sign of good mental and sexual health whether you are 78, 48, or 18. Masturbation affirms the value of your body and pleasure. Masturbation reinforces sexual autonomy and health.
25. Erotic fantasies are used by men and women during couple sex. Erotic fantasies serve as a bridge to sexual desire, arousal, and orgasm. Fantasies are not meant to be acted out, nor are they a sign of what you really want in your sexual relationship. What serves as an erotic charge in fantasy is very different than your actual sexual experience. People who act out erotic fantasies often find it is a "sexual dud". Integrated eroticism fits in the desire/pleasure/eroticism/satisfaction mantra. Accept erotic fantasy as part of integrated eroticism.
26. Sexuality has a 15–20% role in energizing your bond and reinforcing feelings of desire and desirability. Sex is not the chief factor in marriage, but is an integral component. It is even more important for older couples because it reinforces your need for each other. Sexuality and aging is an affirmation of being an engaged, vital couple. There is pride in "beating the odds" and being intimate and erotic friends.

There are many more sexual myths, but fortunately even more healthy sexual understandings. Psychological, biomedical, and social/relational factors promote couple sexuality with aging. Knowledge is power. The more you accept scientifically and clinically relevant understandings the easier it is to enjoy sexuality with aging.

Nancy and Marv

Nancy, who is 71, and 74-year-old Marv have been married 49 years. They have three adult children and five grandchildren, none of whom talked to them about sexual issues. This is a shame because Nancy and Marv are proud of being an aging sexual couple who would like to be life and sex educators.

Marv has positive memories of sexuality during the early years of marriage. Nancy also has happy memories, but feels their present sexual relationship is the most satisfying. Although she'd always enjoyed couple sexuality, she feels it is more genuine now because Marv needs her stimulation. He had not needed her sexually in their younger years. She'd viewed Marv as the more sexually focused partner who almost never passed up a sexual opportunity. She was used to his easy, predictable erections. He always orgasmed during intercourse with his first erection. Now arousal and orgasm are easier for Nancy than Marv. She enjoys that he piggy-backs his arousal on hers. In the last three years Marv has learned to enjoy variable, flexible couple sexuality. Ten years ago he fought against that and tried a number of interventions (Viagra, Cialis, testosterone, a penile pump, a rigorous physical training program) to return him to youthful sex performance. His gift to himself (and Nancy) for his 71st birthday was to adopt GES as his "north star". Marv is grateful that Nancy did not berate him or give up on him. She urges him to enjoy GES.

Although they celebrated mutual, synchronous sexual encounters, they also enjoy asynchronous sexual experiences (although with different preferences). Nancy enjoys self-entrancement arousal, preferring to be the receiver. She can let go and celebrate her orgasmic pattern with Marv's manual stimulation. At other times, she enjoys pleasuring Marv to orgasm with her hand and mouth. Marv much prefers partner interaction arousal with her arousal facilitating his. He jokes that her being so easily orgasmic is compensation for their 20s and 30s when he was the initiator and sex was better for him. Pleasuring Nancy to orgasm is a major turn-on for Marv.

Nancy jokes that having a vibrant sexual life is one of the unexpected surprises about aging. She continues to work 20 hours a week, enjoying the camaraderie of office friendships. The additional income allows them to travel. Marv was pressured to retire nine years earlier. Now he volunteers for a community group which helps older people remain in their homes. Awareness that he "beat the odds" and continues to enjoy sexuality is a source of pride for Marv. For Nancy, sexuality reinforces attachment and energy.

Interestingly, they have separate internists who take a very different approach to sexual issues. Marv's internist encourages him to try new medications which purport to enhance sexual function, but never directly asks Marv about his sex function. Nancy's internist asks a number of questions about her and Marv's quality of life and probes Nancy about mood and anxiety issues, but never mentions sexuality. Each likes their internist, but if they were to experience sexual problems, they would seek a sex therapist and/or a sexual medicine specialist.

Marv and Nancy have an agreement that if they go more than two weeks without a sexual encounter Nancy will initiate a non-demand pleasuring date. This agreement works well. Nancy is pleased she has the role of sexual initiator.

A potential problem involves the role of intercourse. Intercourse had always been more important for Marv than Nancy. She enjoys intercourse, but it never played the core role it had for Marv. At some point, whether two or 15 years in the future, they might have to stop intercourse because of Marv's erections, Nancy's sexual pain, or impaired movement. Nancy would miss intercourse but knows they can enjoy sexuality without intercourse. Marv enjoys erotic and playful sexuality. The question is whether he could accept the cessation of intercourse. This is a challenge for most couples but becomes more common among couples in their 80s. Nancy hopes her sexual enthusiasm will win Marv over if the time comes.

Exercise: Accepting and Enjoying Sexuality in Your 60s, 70s, and 80s

Psychosexual skill exercises integrate and implement concepts in a personal and concrete manner. Changing attitudes and feelings is easier when you have a specific behavioral task to focus on.

In this exercise we ask each of you to make a list. The first list includes attitudes, behaviors, emotions, and values which promote sexuality with aging. Don't be "politically correct" or give socially desirable answers. What is true for you? Examples include enjoying showering or bathing together so you are fresh for oral sexuality, having the freedom to be sexual before or after a nap, a couple weekend at a rustic cabin, taking advantage of slower sexual response to enjoy sensual and playful touching, taking pride in beating the odds, feeling free to wear purple or other non-conventional clothing, watching an erotic DVD or reading a sexy novel, taking a break in the middle of lovemaking for a glass of wine, freedom to masturbate without feeling self-conscious, experimenting with role enactment arousal or sex toys, celebrating the security of your relationship whether it's been three years or 55 years.

Share your lists and note similarities and differences. Similarities acknowledge shared values and experiences. Differences make it clear you are not clones of each other and add spice to your relationship.

The second list is what you plan to do in the next year to enhance desire/pleasure/eroticism/satisfaction. Each partner lists at least one and up to three scenarios or techniques to try. What would add to your experience of sexuality and aging? Each partner has the power to veto a scenario or technique. Unless you have the power to say no to sex you don't have the freedom to say yes to sex. Vetoes are honored, but don't allow this to result in avoidance. Emotionally and physically turn toward your partner and stay engaged.

Commit to add at least two scenarios to your sexual repertoire in the next year. You can't rest on your laurels. Continue to promote intimacy, pleasuring, and eroticism. Remember, you are a sexual person until the day you die.

Who We Are and the Format of this Book

Barry and Emily McCarthy are a husband and wife writing team; this is our 16th co-authored book. When we married in 1966 the male–female double standard was dominant. We were the first in our families to graduate college. We were committed to living our lives in a healthier manner than our family and cultural backgrounds. We wanted to create a life we would be proud of personally and maritally. However, we assumed that sexually we would follow a traditional path. Fortunately, we challenged that assumption and committed to creating a satisfying, secure, and sexual marriage. We are not clones of each other. We are partners who affirm desire/pleasure/eroticism/satisfaction. We have been married 54 years—Barry is 77 and Emily 75. We have three children and three grandchildren.

This book has been a joy to write. We are advocates for sexuality and aging. We are pro-female, pro-male, pro-couple, and pro-sexual. Scientifically, clinically, and personally we advocate for the female–male sexual equity model.

We respect each other's contributions. Emily's background is in speech communication and her writing and wisdom provide a balanced, humanistic perspective. Barry's background is a professor of psychology and a clinical psychologist with a specialty in sex and couple therapy. This book is written for the public, specifically those over age 60. We utilize scientifically and clinically validated psychological, biomedical, and social/relational understandings to promote sexuality. Knowledge is power. We want to motivate and empower you to embrace couple sexuality in your 60s, 70s, and 80s.

We provide scientifically and clinically relevant information and guidelines, psychosexual skill exercises, and case studies (we use composite cases with details altered to protect confidentiality) to make concepts personal and concrete. This book is not meant to be read as a textbook; each chapter is self-contained. Read chapters that are personally relevant. The material can be read for information and concepts but is most valuable as an interactive learning medium. Sharing with your spouse (especially engaging in the exercises) makes the learning personal and meaningful. Implement relevant information, strategies, skills, guidelines, and coping techniques so that sexuality has a 15–20% role in your life and relationship.

This book emphasizes traditional heterosexual married couples. However, most of the concepts and understandings are relevant to partnered relationships as well as lesbian and gay couples. There is a chapter for single people. We are strong advocates for sexual diversity. Sexually, one size never fits all. Rather than use "he" or "she" we utilize "you" when possible to emphasize the female–male equity model and to make concepts personally relevant.

This is a self-help book based on ideas, guidelines, and exercises. It is not a "do-it-yourself" therapy book. The more information, understanding, and resources, the more likely you will make "wise" sexual decisions. Appendix A provides guidelines on how to choose a sex, couple, or individual therapist.

Summary

The prevalence and power of myths about sex and aging is astonishing. Old myths based on lack of knowledge and repressive attitudes die hard. Conservative people and cultures cling to these with the mistaken belief that they are good for couples and the culture. The fear is sexuality will destabilize your lives and marriage. Your sexuality need not be driven by fear.

New sex myths are promoted by the media and the internet. They are based on the demand for sex performance and erotic perfectionism. These sex myths are intimidating. They promise extraordinary sex each and every time. The new myths cause you to feel inferior. The message is you are not "good enough" sexually.

You owe it to yourself, your partner, and your relationship to confront myths, increase sexual understanding and awareness, and enjoy sexuality in your 60s, 70s, and 80s.

2

EMBRACING THE NEW NORMAL: VARIABLE, FLEXIBLE COUPLE SEXUALITY

Sexuality in your 60s, 70s, and 80s is based on pleasure-oriented touching. Be aware of the multiple roles, meanings, and outcomes of couple sexuality. Rather than the traditional routine of foreplay to get the woman ready for intercourse, followed by thrusting with the goal of orgasm during intercourse for both partners, the new sexual model focuses on giving and receiving pleasure-oriented touching. Emphasize sensual, playful, and erotic scenarios in addition to intercourse, utilize multiple stimulation before and during intercourse, realize not all touching will end in intercourse, and the importance of afterplay to ensure satisfaction. The new sexual normal with aging is challenging. Variable, flexible couple sexuality promotes human and satisfying sexuality.

The challenge is more daunting for the man. Unfortunately, many men choose to avoid this challenge and instead give up sex. You say to yourself, "I don't want to start something I can't finish". This is a costly and unwise choice for the man, woman, and couple. You make the choice unilaterally and convey it non-verbally. It results in the cessation of all sensual and sexual touching, not just intercourse. If you asked your partner, she would not agree to stop touching and sexuality. You lose a crucial component of your relationship. Few older couples divorce (although that occurs more frequently), but you lose an important source of intimacy and vitality.

Embracing the new sexual normal is a healthy decision for you and your relationship. Adopt a variable, flexible approach to sexuality involving sensual, playful, and erotic touching. A core change is embracing the Good Enough Sex (GES) approach focused on giving and receiving pleasure rather than clinging to sex as an individual intercourse performance (Metz & McCarthy, 2012). Aging couples value intercourse, but not as a pass–fail test. When sex does not flow to intercourse do not panic or apologize. Turn toward your partner to share sensuality or eroticism whether synchronous or asynchronous. Variable, flexible sex recognizes that sexuality can have a number of roles, meanings, and outcomes. You give up the total predictability of intercourse, replacing it with challenge and pleasure. Usually the encounter flows to intercourse, but not with certainty. Sensual, playful, and erotic scenarios are valuable even when they do not culminate in intercourse. The core dimension in GES is accepting the sexual experience for what it is rather than what it isn't. Sexuality that flows to intercourse is valued, as is sexuality that does not include intercourse. The challenge, especially for the man, is accepting and enjoying non-intercourse sexuality. Accept responsive sexual desire and the importance of sensual, playful, and erotic touch. You give up the demand for easy, predictable erection and intercourse. Enjoy sexual experiences focused on pleasurable touch.

Why is this easier for the woman than the man? For most women sexuality has been variable and flexible throughout your life. Remember, one in three women are never or almost never orgasmic during intercourse (Graham, 2014). You accept that sex is interactive rather than autonomous. It is normal for sexual experiences to include occasional problems with desire, arousal, orgasm, or pain. Variable, flexible GES is congruent with your lived sexual experiences. Men cling to the notion that "real sex" is autonomous erection and intercourse. This worked in your 20s and 30s, although we do not believe it was a healthy learning (McCarthy & McCarthy, 2021). The individual performance model is self-defeating for men in their 60s. The wise man adopts the new normal of variable, flexible sexual response. GES promotes male, female, and couple sexuality in your 60s, 70s, and 80s.

The Challenges and Benefits of the New Normal

Aging sexuality is about challenge, not loss. As young adults, both men and women learn a simple approach to sex—real sex is intercourse, you have a spontaneous erection, and foreplay is to get the woman ready for intercourse. Couples have played out this scenario for 20 years or their entire sexual lives. This sexual routine subverts desire and satisfaction. The male–female double standard was better for the man than the woman. The double standard is self-defeating for sexuality and aging. Rather than giving up sex, the challenge is to embrace the new normal of variable, flexible couple sexuality. This is a challenge worth meeting. It not only allows you to remain sexual, it introduces an added dimension to couple sexuality. Variable, flexible sexuality is more human, genuine, and unpredictable than the traditional foreplay/intercourse routine. Sexual satisfaction is enhanced as both partners acknowledge desire/pleasure/eroticism/satisfaction. Most important is adopting the female–male sexual equity model to replace the double standard. With aging, you are a genuine intimate sexual team who value pleasure. This is the foundation for sexuality with aging. Responsive sexual desire (for both the woman and man) becomes more common than spontaneous desire. Although arousal, intercourse, and orgasm are important, the core value is pleasure-oriented touching. Total predictability is replaced by GES which recognizes the multiple roles, meanings, and outcomes of couple sexuality.

The best sex is mutual and synchronous. Most sexual encounters are asynchronous (positive but better for one partner). A challenge with aging is to accept that often the sexual experience is better for the woman than the man. This can enhance couple sexuality rather than being a loss.

A core understanding is that with aging, sexuality is more human. You need each other more than at any time in your sexual relationship. This includes sensual and playful touching to facilitate desire, willingness and openness to a sexual encounter, receptivity and responsivity to giving and receiving pleasurable touching, utilizing personal and couple erotic scenarios, multiple stimulation (including private erotic fantasies) before intercourse, transitioning to intercourse at high levels of erotic flow, openness to different intercourse positions and types of thrusting, continuing multiple stimulation during intercourse, enjoying each partner's orgasmic response, and celebrating afterplay. Accept the variability and flexibility of your sexual experience.

Laticia and Raymond

Laticia and Raymond were a proud couple in a nine-year marriage, the second for Laticia and Raymond's third. Laticia was 71 and Raymond 68. They attended couple therapy before marrying to ensure that they created the foundation for a satisfying, secure, and sexual marriage.

Laticia's family and friends were particularly concerned about the marriage. Raymond had a legacy of two bitter ex-wives and three struggling adult children. Raymond had a history of alcohol and drug abuse and was experiencing erectile dysfunction (ED). He regretted a number of things about his past, but "owned" and processed these experiences. Raymond was not ashamed of his history. Most important he was motivated to create a satisfying, secure, and sexual marriage with Laticia. They had a clear agreement to not lie about past or present experiences. Raymond shared themes from his past but was not controlled by the painful details. Processing themes is therapeutic, disclosing all details and obsessing about them is anti-therapeutic and keeps you stuck in the past. A trap for Raymond was feeling embarrassed and regretful about the past. Raymond wanted to be loved for who he really was, not weighed down by history.

Laticia understood and accepted Raymond. Her major vulnerability was fears and distrust that Raymond would have a secret life, especially sexually. They agreed that once a week Raymond would initiate a discussion and let Laticia know if there were problems or sensitive material she needed to be aware of. Raymond taking responsibility for this was crucial. Rather than Laticia being in the role of the hyper-vigilant detective, she and Raymond would process difficult issues.

Laticia and Raymond were committed to establishing and maintaining a satisfying and secure marriage. They wanted to enjoy their aging process. Adopting a variable, flexible approach to sexuality was key. This was particularly important for Raymond. In past relationships ED had been a cue to begin affairs or use paid sex to rebuild sexual confidence. Raymond was committed to turn to Laticia as his intimate and erotic ally in rebuilding comfort and confidence with erections. Adopting GES was key to their sexual relationship. Their favorite milieu to discuss sexual issues was on a hike, stopping at a rock overlooking the valley. They agreed not to talk about sexual problems in bed, especially not after a disappointing sexual encounter. Raymond vividly recalled destructive arguments with other partners after failed intercourse. There is something about being nude in bed after a negative sexual experience which brings out the worst in people.

Laticia and Raymond created scenarios to reinforce variable, flexible couple sexuality. Laticia felt comfortable bringing up sexual issues and creating scenarios. Raymond was open to engage, something he had avoided in previous relationships. He was grateful for Laticia's pro-sexual attitudes and emotions. He was aware that she had felt sexually betrayed in the past. This increased his motivation to keep sexual agreements, especially regarding monogamy. It required Raymond to give up the traditional male privilege of freedom to have sex with other women. Raymond realized that affairs had been costly in his life. They had not built self-esteem nor enhanced erectile confidence. If he had it to do over, he would have chosen a different sexual strategy. At age 68 he could not have a "do over". He could enjoy sexuality with Laticia in the present. She reminded him (and herself) that the power of change is in the present and future (Bethell, 2020).

Raymond was a "wise man" who "beat the odds" and created a healthy sexual relationship with aging. He gave up the goal of reliable, predictable erections, replacing it with a focus on sharing pleasure and eroticism. Raymond was orgasmic in over 95% of sexual encounters whether with intercourse, manual, or oral stimulation. He became comfortable mixing self-stimulation with Laticia's oral stimulation. Although Laticia enjoyed being orgasmic and knew she had a right to orgasm, it was less of a goal. She felt good about a sexual experience whether she was orgasmic or not. A difference in sexual preference was that she valued asynchronous self-entrancement arousal. Raymond enjoyed pleasuring Laticia to orgasm first, but he wanted to be orgasmic during that sexual encounter. On her birthday, Laticia's request was to be "selfish" and not feel responsible for Raymond having an orgasm. She held him while he stimulated himself to orgasm. Being an intimate sexual team does not mean being clones of each other. Laticia and Raymond have the right to their sexual feelings and preferences.

Questions of sexual frequency and initiation are a common source of miscommunication and frustration. Raymond focused on frequency more than Laticia—he feared they would fall into the sexual avoidance trap. He assured Laticia that his initiation was for attachment, not goal-oriented intercourse. A touching date could transition to intercourse, but this was neither a demand nor a pressure. The initiation was an invitation to share pleasure. If the touching led to "responsive sexual desire" which flowed to intercourse that was great. Often responsive desire would transition to a sensual or playful experience which primed them for intercourse in the next day or two. Laticia particularly valued "bridges to desire" which invited a sexual encounter. Her favorite bridge was taking a shower, a 20-minute nap, and waking to Raymond's caressing and oral breast stimulation. Sometimes this transitioned to intercourse, other times it resulted in an erotic scenario to orgasm. A major change is that Raymond was positive about erotic (non-intercourse) scenarios. This was a relief for Laticia who had lobbied for broad-based sexuality. Laticia felt Raymond worried too much about sex. She accepted however the touching experience played out. As long as Laticia felt intimately attached she was fine with less predictable sex.

A crucial issue for all couples, especially aging couples, is how to deal with dissatisfying or dysfunctional encounters. Couples report 5–15% of experiences are problematic (Frank, Anderson, & Rubinstein, 1978). This is higher with older couples. The ideal reaction is to laugh or shrug off the experience and be sexual in the next few days when both partners are comfortable and receptive. Unfortunately, that strategy did not fit for Raymond and Laticia. She took the lead in switching to their "trust position" where they were quiet yet attached. This calmed Raymond and they enjoyed the closeness.

Raymond and Laticia hope to be sexual for the rest of their lives. With a three-year age difference, they wondered who would be the first to die. Many of Laticia's female friends were widows—this is the common pattern and cultural expectation. If she were to be widowed, she would miss the intimacy and touching. Most of Raymond's friends who were widowers remarried, some happily but many not. Raymond would need to be a very lucky man to have a relationship which was as good as the one he experienced with Laticia.

The Role of Afterplay in the New Normal

Traditionally couples had either a short, routine afterplay consisting of a kiss and saying, "I love you", or they ignored afterplay. Variable, flexible afterplay is an integral component of the new normal. You just shared an intense sexual experience, turn toward your partner to bond and share afterplay. Afterplay is important whether the encounter involved intercourse or not, was wonderful or just okay, was synchronous or asynchronous. Afterplay enhances sexuality and is especially important with aging. No matter what the experience, turning toward your partner to share afterplay is bonding and enhances satisfaction.

Afterplay is emotionally affirming and reinforces being an intimate sexual team. Afterplay can be playful, creative, intimate, or cuddly. Usually it lasts two to five minutes, but can be 30 minutes or longer. Afterplay can include an invitation for a second sexual encounter whether mutual or asynchronous. Afterplay is particularly meaningful when the sexual experience was dissatisfying or dysfunctional. The message of afterplay is to affirm being a couple and to end the encounter in a positive manner. A prime message is affirming sexuality with aging. Afterplay can have multiple roles and meanings.

Exercise: Embracing Variable, Flexible Couple Sexuality

This exercise involves more than acceptance. It affirms the variable, flexible approach to couple sexuality with aging. There are two components. First, identify what you value about variable, flexible couple sexuality. Second, develop a specific plan to implement this approach.

Each make a list and then combine them. Examples of advantages of variable, flexible sexuality include:

1. Enjoying sexual unpredictability
2. Spending more time with pleasuring
3. Valuing playful scenarios and techniques
4. Needing each other's touch to facilitate arousal
5. Learning to piggy-back his arousal on hers
6. Engaging in sensual scenarios as part of couple sexuality
7. Realizing that subjective arousal is more important than objective arousal
8. Not feeling pressured by his erection
9. Enjoying asynchronous sexual experiences
10. Celebrating responsive desire
11. Feeling free to choose sexual scenarios and techniques
12. Waiting to transition to intercourse until both partners feel subjective and objective arousal

As you discuss and combine your lists, be sure each partner is genuine in feelings and preferences. Don't give socially desirable answers. For example, we advocate for multiple stimulation before and during intercourse, but some individuals prefer single stimulation. Another example is we advocate for sensual, playful, and erotic sexuality, but some partners are not comfortable with playful scenarios. We advocate for asynchronous sexual scenarios, but some partners find these awkward or intimidating.

Be sure the listed advantages are true for both partners (although it need not be equally positive). Be clear and specific about your preferences.

The second component—implementation—is more challenging yet more important. We suggest scheduling dates to implement your sexual preferences. For example, needing each other's touch to facilitate arousal—set up a sexual date with time to give and receive partner interaction arousal. An involved, aroused partner is the major aphrodisiac. Do you prefer partner interaction arousal, self-entrancement arousal, or role enactment arousal? Create a scenario which uses your preferred arousal style.

Another date involves implementing responsive sexual desire, a bedrock strategy for sexuality and aging. Rather than wait until you feel "horny", pick a time neither partner feels spontaneous desire. What combination of affectionate, sensual, and playful touching is inviting for you? Does silence, small sounds, or talking facilitate sexual openness and willingness? What can you and your partner do to facilitate desire? Is there anything you or your partner do which is a turn-off? If so, drop it from your sexual repertoire.

Build responsive sexual desire to promote couple sexuality (McCarthy & McCarthy, 2012). The crucial learning is that responsive desire is the norm for aging women and men.

Another scenario to implement involves asynchronous sexuality. Asynchronous sexual experiences are healthy as long as it is not at the expense of your partner or relationship. Asynchronous scenarios enhance variable, flexible couple sexuality.

Play out up to three asynchronous scenarios. Be sure you don't feel you're "servicing" the partner or feel manipulated. That builds resentment and undermines desire. Ideally, your partner finds the scenario pleasurable (or at least comfortable). On a 10-point scale of subjective arousal, the asynchronous scenario is at least a 1 and ideally a 5 or 7 for the partner. If it elicits negative feelings drop that scenario.

An example is a self-entrancement scenario where you pleasure your spouse to orgasm. This is a 10 for the receiving partner. The giving partner enjoys feeling in sexual control and the responsivity of the receiving partner. Subjective arousal might be 3 or 6, better for the receiving partner but positive for the giving partner.

An example of an acceptable asynchronous intercourse scenario is when you find it highly erotic to have intercourse in the man-on-top position with her legs up so her feet touch your shoulders. In addition, you use a private fantasy scenario of being fellated by an anonymous 21-year-old "bad girl". Your partner enjoys seeing you swept away with erotic feelings and sensations. For her, the experience is superior to "going along for the ride".

An example of an unacceptable asynchronous scenario is where you find high arousal during intercourse when he provides multiple stimulation by stretching to provide buttock stimulation and, with his body extended, oral breast stimulation. The problem is he experiences painful leg cramps. It is 10 for you, but −4 for him. He is "servicing" you at his expense. That is not what you want. He has a right to eliminate the painful stretching so asynchronous intercourse is positive.

End this exercise by discussing sexual strategies and techniques. Reinforce variable, flexible sexuality with aging for you and your relationship.

Is Variable, Flexible Couple Sexuality Better than Autonomous, Predictable Sex?

The great majority of men learn (and overlearn) that sex function is autonomous, predictable, and centered on intercourse. You have experienced this hundreds of times over the years. Most couples do not value variable, flexible sexuality until they encounter sexual problems. That is sad because we believe that variable, flexible couple sexuality is healthier than predictable, autonomous sex. We wish we had adopted this in our 20s rather than wait until our 50s.

A chief advantage of variable, flexible sexuality is that it reflects the inherent complexity of couple sexuality. It honors the multiple roles, meanings, and outcomes of sexuality. Accept sexual experiences whether wonderful or mediocre. A key is to turn toward your partner rather than avoiding or apologizing. Recognizing complex sexual motivations and outcomes normalizes your sexual experiences.

A core concept is to balance individual autonomy and being an intimate sexual team. Also, the balance between a pleasure orientation and sexual function. Your challenge is to integrate intimacy, pleasuring, and eroticism. Recognize the value of both intercourse and non-intercourse sexuality. Variable, flexible sexuality asks you to integrate intimacy and eroticism; realize they are different but complementary dimensions.

Traditionally, couples place high value on predictable, functional sex. This is a reasonable preference, but a self-defeating demand, especially with aging. Embrace variable, flexible sexuality. Your challenge is to accept less predictable sex. Do you keep trying to make intercourse work every time? Or do you transition to a sensual or erotic scenario, whether synchronous or asynchronous? Embracing GES and enjoying variable, flexible sexuality is not just acceptable, but optimal. Respect individual differences. Some couples would rather "take a raincheck" and be sexual a few days later. Find the best approach for you. We strongly advise against giving up and avoiding sex.

An advantage of sexuality and aging is enjoying the range of sexual roles, meanings, and outcomes. This reinforces sexual vitality. Embrace the humanity of being an aging couple. As one of Barry's clients said, "Sexuality and aging is an adventure".

Summary

The new sexual normal features a focus on pleasure-oriented couple experiences rather than intercourse and orgasm as an individual performance. Variable, flexible couple sexuality emphasizes sensual, playful, and erotic stimulation both before and during intercourse; accepting GES, especially realizing that not all touching will result in intercourse; and integrating afterplay to enhance sexual satisfaction. Embracing variable, flexible couple sexuality with aging is not just accepting but celebrating sexuality. Variable, flexible sex recognizes the range of sexual roles, meanings, and outcomes. Sexuality is more genuine and human than the predictable foreplay, intercourse, and orgasm routine. The best of sexuality, especially satisfaction, reaches fruition with aging.

3

SEXUALITY IS MORE THAN INTERCOURSE: CHALLENGE, NOT LOSS

A key to couple sexuality after 60 is to redefine what you mean by sex. In traditional socialization "sex = intercourse". The new definition of sexuality includes sensual, playful, and erotic scenarios in addition to intercourse. You need to end the traditional male–female power struggle of "intercourse or nothing". Although we advocate for intercourse, it is in the context of sharing pleasure and eroticism, not an individual pass–fail performance test. Accepting and valuing broad-based sexuality is a challenge.

Cultural learnings understand aging through the lens of loss, including sexual loss. We advocate an approach to aging that emphasizes challenge, not loss (Bethell, 2020). This is true of sexuality generally and intercourse specifically.

There are two core issues regarding intercourse. First, redefine sexuality as involving sensual, playful, and erotic scenarios. In Chapter 2 we emphasized the importance of variable, flexible couple sexual experiences. The challenge for both partners is to embrace this expanded view of sexuality. It adds to the vitality of your sexual relationship, and its importance cannot be overstated. Second, if one or both partners can no longer engage in intercourse is it possible to continue to enjoy couple sexuality? We believe that sexuality without intercourse is not only possible, but can provide the 15–20% role of energizing your bond and reinforcing feelings of desire and desirability. Embracing non-intercourse sexuality is a major couple challenge.

Couples have positive memories and feelings about intercourse whether for 30 years or 50 years. You enjoyed predictable, functional intercourse as well as "foreplay" and "fooling around". Intercourse was the "main event". Some couples emphasized manual, oral, rubbing, or vibrator stimulation as a way to enhance arousal and orgasm, especially for the woman. For the man, unless you had intercourse it wasn't sex. You learned this as an adolescent and had it reinforced for more than 50 years. However, this demand subverts couple sexuality with aging. Male peers, physicians, and drug company salesmen reinforce the self-defeating pressure for intercourse. This intercourse demand eventually leads to a non-sexual relationship. Typically, your partner urges you to embrace a broad approach to sexuality. This crucial dialogue is avoided because it is such a complex, emotionally challenging topic. Your challenge is to successfully implement non-intercourse sexuality. A broad, flexible couple sexual repertoire is of great value. Sadly, most couples allow touching and sex to stop. A very unwise choice personally and relationally.

It takes personal and couple courage to dialogue, play out, and embrace sensual, playful, and erotic sexuality. It does not happen automatically. Throughout this book we emphasize being intimate and erotic allies who turn toward each other and share pleasure. The most challenging issue is embracing non-intercourse sexuality. This is easier if you have a history of variable, flexible sexual expression. A pattern for many couples was the woman being aroused and orgasmic with manual, oral, rubbing, or vibrator stimulation before (or after) intercourse and the man being orgasmic during intercourse. These learnings make it easier to transition to him being orgasmic with erotic stimulation. A key for implementation is to practice the psychosexual skill exercises in this chapter. Reading and talking are of great value, but the real change comes with implementing the psychosexual skill exercises. You agree to not have intercourse even if one or both partners are eager to. This is a crucial emotional commitment. It allows you to experiment with sensual, playful, and especially erotic scenarios. The value of non-intercourse sexuality becomes personal and concrete. In this learning process, you are not using sensual or erotic scenarios because intercourse was unsuccessful. You are affirmatively exploring non-intercourse strategies and techniques to enhance desire and satisfaction.

Exercise: Exploring Non-Intercourse Sexuality

This exercise requires both partners to engage in a "good faith" exploration of non-intercourse sexual expression. Not only is there a prohibition on intercourse but, more important, openness to exploring sensual, playful, and erotic scenarios and techniques.

Set aside at least 45 minutes. We suggest taking a shower or bath and beginning with affectionate and sensual touch. Enjoy each other's bodies, but don't include genital touch. Dry your partner's body. Do not go to your bedroom, but to your favorite room in the house. An advantage of aging is you have private space, you are not worried about children interrupting. Be sexual in the guest bedroom, den, or living room. Be sure you have privacy and are not interrupted—turn off your cell phone and don't answer the door. Do you prefer touching and being touched (partner interaction arousal) or taking turns where one is the giver and the other the receiver (self-entrancement arousal)? The focus of sensual touch is subjective arousal in the 1–3 range. This is the basis of sensate focus (Weiner & Avery-Clark, 2017). Identify what is pleasurable—back rub with your eyes closed, giving pleasurable touch, or holding and caressing. Often, your preferences are different than your partner's. Not only is that acceptable, it is good to add variety to your sexual relationship. Sensual sexuality is different than intercourse. It adds a special dimension to couple sexuality.

At a different time and setting explore playful scenarios. In terms of subjective arousal playful touch is in the 4–5 range. Playful scenarios intermix non-genital and genital pleasuring which can involve taking turns or mutual touching. Women find playful touch particularly inviting because it is so different than goal-oriented foreplay. Enjoy being active rather than passive. Being sexual in a playful manner is energizing. Playful touch is valued for itself rather than a substitute because you can't have intercourse. This provides an important learning about valuing both synchronous and asynchronous encounters. We usually advocate for synchronous sexuality, but not in this situation. As you explore playful scenarios it is common that one partner (often the woman) particularly enjoys asynchronous sexuality. Traditionally, the man's arousal/erection was viewed as a demand for intercourse or at least an orgasm. In playful scenarios, there is no expectation of orgasm—enjoy playful touching for itself. It is likely to be better for one partner.

Erotic, non-intercourse scenarios are the most challenging. Subjective arousal feelings and sensations are in the 6–10 range. You can let eroticism flow to orgasm or continue a prohibition on orgasm. Enjoy the erotic scenario for itself, not as a substitute for intercourse. Erotic scenarios can involve manual, oral, rubbing, or vibrator stimulation or a combination of these.

Our suggestion is to have a prohibition on orgasm for the first erotic scenario. This is not to be "politically correct", but to give you the opportunity to enjoy erotic feelings and sensations. Orgasm is a natural result of pleasure/eroticism/erotic flow, not to prove something to yourself or your partner. Explore erotic techniques and feelings, whether twice or three times. This reinforces vital sexuality without performance demands. Couples in therapy have told Barry this made the concepts they'd read about and discussed personally meaningful. Erotic scenarios clarify dimensions of sexuality and aging.

Next, integrate orgasm into your erotic scenario. For most couples, stimulating your partner to orgasm (whether the man or woman) is goal-oriented. In this exercise we encourage a pleasure-oriented approach to eroticism and orgasm. Try this first with manual stimulation, next with oral stimulation, and then with your preferred mix of stimulation. Try mutual (partner interaction) and taking turns (self-entrancement). This is not a matter of "right-wrong" or "perfect", but what is erotic for you. Pleasuring/eroticism flows to orgasm, rather than working to achieve orgasm. Orgasm is integral to the desire/pleasure/eroticism/satisfaction mantra.

The last component in this exercise involves afterplay. Traditionally, afterplay had been a perfunctory ritual. This exercise gives you the power to explore afterplay scenarios and techniques after a non-intercourse encounter. Afterplay has meaning whether the encounter was sensual, playful, or erotic. Afterplay is important whether or not the encounter was wonderful or disappointing. Instead of a perfunctory "I love you" and a kiss, explore involving and meaningful afterplay scenarios. Afterplay can be synchronous or asynchronous, verbal or non-verbal, intimate or playful, last for two minutes or 20 minutes, involve caressing or tickling, reinforce bonding or be energizing.

Developing and implementing afterplay scenarios enhances your experience, especially satisfaction. We encourage you to explore "his", "hers", and "our" afterplay scenarios. What is a good fit for you? You don't need intercourse or orgasm to enjoy afterplay. Afterplay has value with sensual, playful, and erotic experiences.

The theme of this exercise is acceptance of the range of non-intercourse sexuality. This is a challenge. Your sexuality, personally and as a couple, is not contingent on intercourse.

Affirming Pleasure-Oriented Touching

Pleasure-oriented touch is the essence of couple sexuality. Sexuality does not stop when you stop intercourse. Sexuality does stop when you stop touching. We describe five dimensions (gears) of touch: affection, sensual, playful, erotic, and intercourse. Affection is crucial, but affectionate touch is not sexual. Intercourse is an important part of sexual touch but doesn't define sexual touch. Most couples, especially men, do not easily accept the cessation of intercourse, but acceptance can be the best decision. By the time couples stop intercourse, the intercourse experience is no longer enjoyable. The positive anticipation, pleasure-oriented touch, eroticism leading to intercourse, enjoying ejaculation, and feeling energized and bonded has become a distant memory. The intercourse experience is controlled by anticipatory and performance anxiety with a rush to intercourse. Intercourse is more a relief than a joy. Often the outcome is frustration, embarrassment, and angst. Intercourse has become a performance-oriented chore.

Couples who embrace sensual, playful, and erotic sexuality say they should have dropped intercourse two or even ten years before. Your sexual relationship was burdened by intercourse, not energized by it.

For most couples, the transition from predictable intercourse to irregular intercourse to intercourse failure and avoidance occurs gradually over years. However, some couples experience dramatic change over weeks or months. You become stuck in the cycle of anticipatory anxiety, tense sex, rushing to intercourse driven by fear of failure, frustration, and embarrassment eventually leading to avoidance. This controls male and couple sexuality. We are pro-intercourse, but the pass–fail performance approach robs intercourse of intimacy and pleasure. You want to keep intercourse in your sexual repertoire. This is healthy as long as both partners are aware that there is sexuality beyond intercourse.

Female Sexual Pain with Intercourse

Although we focus on ED as the prime cause for stopping sex, it is not the only factor. A major problem is female genital pain generally and pain during intercourse specifically. There is a large clinical literature on managing sexual pain (Bergeron, Rosen, Pukall, & Corsini-Munt, 2020). The goal is increased sexual awareness and comfort. The emphasis is on sexual involvement, touch, and pleasure. Don't demand pain-free intercourse (perfectionistic and unrealistic), but enjoyment of the sexual experience, including intercourse. Use a variety of coping resources to build comfort. With aging these techniques become less efficacious and intercourse can become an aversive activity. Intercourse should not be at the expense of female pain. Rather than "intercourse or nothing", as intimate and erotic allies you create a vital and satisfying non-intercourse sexual style. Some couples prefer rubbing between her thighs or rubbing his penis against her breasts. Other couples utilize anal intercourse if the man has a firm erection. Like couples dealing with ED, you utilize manual, oral, rubbing, or vibrator stimulation. You intermix sensual and playful stimulation. Many find asynchronous scenarios satisfying. The message is that sexuality is about sharing pleasure, not clinging to intercourse.

Recognize that with aging many women (and men) find it easier to be orgasmic with manual, oral, or rubbing stimulation. The challenge is to explore and experiment. Discover what promotes desire/pleasure/eroticism/satisfaction for each partner. Developing a vital, satisfying sexuality is best approached as a couple challenge.

Another strategy involves self-stimulation during couple sex. This is quite different than masturbation, which is a solitary experience. Self-stimulation during partner sexuality is a way to build erotic flow to orgasm. For example, the man does oral breast stimulation and manual vulva stimulation while she engages in manual or vibrator clitoral stimulation. Or the man does penile stimulation while the woman kisses him and engages in testicle stimulation. Multiple stimulation, including self-stimulation, becomes more common with aging. Psychologically, the important distinction is increased involvement in pleasuring and eroticism, not working to prove something sexually.

Variable, flexible couple sexuality challenges the routine of intercourse sex. Sexuality involving unpredictability and experimentation is very different than routine, predictable intercourse. Include intercourse in the sexual mix, but not as the only way to be sexual. Pleasure and acceptance take the starring role.

Rex and Jaline

Friends and adult children admired and even envied 78-year-old Rex and 72-year-old Jaline. This was a 17-year second marriage for both. They dealt with a number of physical health and financial issues that would demoralize other couples. Jaline and Rex had a solid guideline "Focus on what you can control and accept what you can't control". Jaline was a breast cancer survivor who had been forced to retire early due to rheumatoid arthritis. Rex experienced ED in his first marriage, beginning at age 43, caused by poorly controlled diabetes. Jaline encouraged him to be physically healthy which resulted in significantly improved diabetic control, but only minimal change in erectile function. Rex was a retired police officer, but because of poor management of retirement funds by the city, his pension was significantly reduced. Jaline and Rex realized that medical and financial problems would continue to impact their lives. Although unfair, this was an unchangeable reality. What they could control was the quality of their relationship, especially couple sexuality. Rex was more likely to engage in "what if" thinking. Jaline reminded him to stay focused on the things he could control. Rex particularly enjoyed that he had "beaten the odds" and was sexual when the majority of male peers had given up sex.

A key was embracing sensual, playful, and erotic sexuality. Jaline had no problem with giving up intercourse. Throughout her sexual life, she found erotic sexuality more satisfying than intercourse. Her first husband and other partners focused on intercourse. Men treated Jaline's inability to be orgasmic during intercourse as her problem. Jaline viewed men as sexually selfish, judgmental, and unaware of female anatomy and physiology. In contrast, from the beginning Rex was attentive to her sexual feelings. Although Rex's motivations were not healthy (he was apologetic about ED), he enjoyed pleasuring Jaline to orgasm. This allowed her to experience pleasure and orgasm in a manner she had not before. Her sexual response pattern involved kissing, oral breast stimulation, and manual clitoral stimulation. She had a strong preference for self-entrancement arousal rather than partner interaction arousal. Rex enjoyed being the giving partner. He was turned-on when she verbalized "that feels so good". The disconnect occurred when he broke her erotic flow by trying to initiate intercourse. Although some of the time he was able to enter her, he would lose his erection. His panicking and apologizing were anti-erotic. What had begun as a positive experience for both ended in an alienating manner.

Over the years Rex had consulted a number of urologists. He'd tried Viagra, Cialis, Levitra, testosterone enhancement, and penile injections. Finally, he was referred to a urologist/surgeon who recommended a penile prosthesis. Jaline had been supportive on this medical odyssey, but finally said "enough is enough". Their sexual life had a dramatic split—pleasuring and eroticism were exciting and energizing, intercourse was frustrating and alienating. Rex's approach to intercourse was self-defeating. Jaline was turned-off by the penile injections. Although it produced a firm erection, Rex did not want to be touched nor did he want to touch her. He rushed to intercourse and struggled to reach orgasm. He was objectively aroused (erection), but not subjectively aroused. Jaline described this as "canoeing against the current". Intercourse was not enjoyable for either partner. A penile prosthesis would make intercourse even more of a performance. Penile prosthesis is an irreversible medical procedure. She feared Rex's ED was driving them into a dead-end which would destroy couple sexuality.

Rather than seeking a second medical opinion, Jaline lobbied to consult a couple sex therapist. The therapist utilized a four-session assessment model (McCarthy & Ross, 2017). The first session is conducted as a couple to reinforce that sexuality is a couple issue. The second and third sessions are individual psychological/relational/sexual histories. These individual sessions were crucial. Jaline emphasized how much she enjoyed self-entrancement arousal, but mistakenly believed that Rex did not enjoy being the giving partner. She did not understand his approach to erection and intercourse. She had never told Rex how badly she felt for him when he tried to force intercourse. She was afraid Rex would be devasted if she were sexually honest. She feared he would view her as sexually selfish and not loving him—the opposite of her genuine feelings.

It was even more difficult for Rex to talk about his feelings and concerns. He mistakenly believed that Jaline needed intercourse sex. He was aware that she was responsive and orgasmic with manual stimulation, but mistakenly believed she needed orgasm during intercourse. Rex disliked the mechanical nature of the penile injection and did not enjoy intercourse even when he achieved intromission. Thrusting was like climbing a steep mountain. Even when you reach the top (orgasm) it was more of a relief than a joy. When the clinician asked Rex about masturbation, he was embarrassed to disclose he was orgasmic over 70% of the time. He felt guilty about masturbation, and feared Jaline would be very upset that Rex masturbated one to two times a week. Rex was burdened by confusing and shameful secrets.

The clinician tells each client you can "red-flag" sensitive material. Sensitive issues are not shared with the spouse without your permission. The clinician usually lobbies the client(s) to share sensitive information because it is crucial to the acceptance and change process. This was true for both Jaline and Rex. Jaline easily gave permission because she wanted to process psychological and sexual issues. Rex was reluctant because he felt shameful and feared her judgment. The clinician assured Rex that this material would be processed in a therapeutic manner.

The 90-minute couple feedback session was a turning point for Jaline and Rex. The clinician was empathic and respectful, but clear they needed a new approach to desire/pleasure/eroticism/satisfaction. Penile prosthesis surgery was the wrong way to go. Rex was tearful and felt relieved.

The therapeutic strategy was restoring intimacy, pleasuring, and eroticism. Rex did not have to prove himself with erection and intercourse. Jaline made it clear that she enjoyed pleasuring and eroticism, she didn't need intercourse. For Jaline intercourse was not a valued activity. This was a shock to Rex. He hadn't enjoyed the erection/intercourse struggle for years, including before he met Jaline. They should have had this conversation years ago. The clinician wanted to be sure this would be a clear, empowering dialogue.

Jaline wanted Rex to accept that her "sexual voice" and orgasmic response was with manual stimulation. She was not anti-intercourse, but intercourse only made sense if it was valued by Rex. It was now clear to both that this was not the reality. The clinician asked Rex whether he enjoyed being orgasmic with her stimulation. They had never engaged in this conversation. The only way he had been orgasmic with Jaline was during intercourse or rubbing against her when intercourse failed. He had never allowed her to stimulate him to orgasm. She assumed that this was his preference. A good example that our assumptions are often wrong.

With his permission, the clinician disclosed that Rex was regularly orgasmic with masturbation. Rex was expecting to be rebuked. Instead, Jaline was enthusiastic about pleasuring Rex to orgasm. Jaline wanted Rex to understand that she valued couple sexuality, especially self-entrancement arousal/eroticism scenarios. She wanted Rex to enjoy couple sexuality. This was something they could change and control. Rex needed to view pleasure and eroticism as a shared domain. Jaline was his intimate and erotic friend.

Jaline and Rex talked about sexual scenarios and techniques in therapy and at home. Since self-entrancement arousal worked so well for her, she believed it would work for Rex. Although he appreciated her sexual responsivity, Rex had his own sexual preferences. Rex learned to piggy-back his arousal on Jaline's. He used self-stimulation to enhance subjective and objective arousal. Once he felt subjectively aroused, he was responsive to Jaline's combination of manual and oral stimulation. Rex was feeling better about sexuality than at any time in his adult life. This was the best sex they had experienced in 17 years as a couple. Neither missed intercourse. Dropping intercourse was the right decision. It freed them, especially Rex, to experience erotic scenarios and techniques.

Jaline and Rex agreed to six-month follow-up sessions for at least a year. They had come a long way and would not permit a relapse. Jaline made it clear that if Rex wanted to reestablish intercourse, she was willing, but valued broad-based erotic sexuality and did not need intercourse. Rex was confident and satisfied with erotic sexuality. Although he would not say never to intercourse, he did not miss the intercourse struggles.

Valuing Sexuality Without Intercourse

The message of this chapter is complex and nuanced. We advocate variable, flexible couple sexuality and redefining sex to include sensual, playful, and erotic sexuality. We strongly advocate for GES which recognizes the multiple roles, meanings, and outcomes of couple sexuality. The positive, realistic expectation is that 85% of encounters flow to intercourse. When sex does not result in intercourse you transition to a sensual or erotic scenario. This gives intercourse a positive role in couple sexuality, but it no longer has the dominant or necessary role. Embrace variable, flexible sexuality.

The challenge is to value sexuality that does not include intercourse. Men and women accept the cessation of intercourse with sadness, but this does not negate desire/pleasure/eroticism/satisfaction. Sexuality continues to have a 15–20% role for you and your relationship. Recognize the value of sensual, playful, and especially erotic touching. Touch and pleasure are the essence of sexuality with aging. Accept the challenge of being intimate and erotic allies, enjoy feelings of attachment, and embrace a variety of sensual and sexual experiences. Rather than loss, acknowledge good memories of intercourse, while celebrating pleasure-oriented couple sexuality.

Summary

It is freeing to reject the definition of sex as a pass–fail intercourse test. Embrace sexuality which involves sensual, playful, and erotic touching in addition to intercourse. Although many couples continue to enjoy intercourse into their 80s, a significant number find intercourse is no longer anticipated or enjoyable whether because of erectile dysfunction, genital pain, or other biomedical problems. The challenge is to accept the cessation of intercourse while continuing to enjoy broad-based, variable, flexible sexuality. You are proud to "beat the odds" and be a "wise man" rather than a traditional man who defines sex as intercourse. The woman's experience of intimate, interactive couple sexuality is validated with aging. Sexuality is more human. You feel needed in a way you hadn't 20 years before. Couple sexuality is more satisfying with aging. Sexuality is in the context of sharing pleasure and eroticism, not an individual performance. Embrace sexuality as a pleasure-oriented challenge, not intercourse as a loss.

4

GOOD ENOUGH SEX (GES): ROLES, MEANINGS, AND OUTCOMES

A key for sexuality and aging is embracing Good Enough Sex (GES). Traditionally, intercourse and orgasm were the measure of sex. Sex was a simple pass–fail test. Orgasm must occur during intercourse for both women and men. The belief was the height of sexual satisfaction was simultaneous orgasm.

The focus on individual performance was easier for the man than the woman. The most common male sex dysfunction was premature ejaculation. The assumption (which is not scientifically true) was that prolonged intercourse was how women reached orgasm.

In 2007, Michael Metz introduced a positive, realistic couple approach to sexuality—GES (Metz & McCarthy, 2007). GES recognizes that by its nature couple sexuality is variable, flexible, and complex. There are two major premises for GES. First, sexuality is a couple process of sharing pleasure, not an individual sex performance. Second, sexuality has a range of roles, meanings, and outcomes. GES affirms the complexity and meaning of couple sexuality rather than a simplistic, "We had sex".

GES is easier for women to accept than men because it is congruent with female sexual socialization and lived sexual experiences. There is little support for GES from male peers, doctors, or drug company salesmen. The woman adopting GES encourages the man to enjoy sexuality with aging. You are a "wise" man who values sexuality in your 60s, 70s, and 80s. Traditional men stop being sexual in their 50s and 60s because you have lost confidence in totally predictable erection and intercourse.

Embracing GES is the "wise" decision for men, women, couples, and the culture. GES enhances sexuality in your 60s, 70s, and 80s.

Since its introduction, GES has been a source of much contention. Sex educators and clinicians advocate GES as a positive, realistic model for men and couples. Metz & McCarthy (2012) advocated for GES as an empowering and motivating model. However, male physicians, especially urologists, have not been supportive. They argue that biomedical interventions can restore men to perfect sex function rather than "settling for GES". GES is compatible with medical interventions, especially pro-erection medications, as well as testosterone enhancement and the penile pump. The issue is whether the medical intervention is viewed as a stand-alone approach to restore you to guaranteed sex performance. There is little scientific evidence to support this for middle-years men and no evidence for men after 60 (Althof, 2006). GES is a couple approach focused on sharing pleasure rather than individual performance. GES is anti-perfectionistic. Even the physically healthiest 60-year-old man in a wonderful relationship realizes it is unrealistic to hope that you will always have an erection sufficient for intercourse. In reality, whether once a year or once a month, it is normal to experience unsuccessful intercourse. This is not acceptable in the individual performance model, but is compatible with GES. The guideline in GES is that 85% of sexual encounters will flow from comfort to pleasure to arousal to erotic flow to intercourse to orgasm. When sexuality does not flow, you transition to a sensual or erotic scenario or agree to take a "rain check" (Metz & McCarthy, 2004). You return to intercourse in the next few days when feeling receptive and responsive. GES is motivating and empowering for both men and women.

GES and Aging

GES is particularly relevant for couples over 60. It ensures sexuality will continue to thrive with aging. Clinging to the individual pass–fail intercourse model makes it likely that you will stop sex because you lose confidence in totally predictable erection and intercourse. You make this choice unilaterally and convey it non-verbally by ignoring sexual touching. The essence of GES is a couple process of giving and receiving pleasure-oriented touching. GES affirms that sensual, playful, and erotic scenarios are sexual in addition to intercourse. The most important GES component is establishing positive, realistic expectations while confronting perfectionistic performance demands. This is especially important for sexuality and aging, but is relevant for couples of all ages, orientations, and levels of relationship. Media depictions and porn videos advocate for a dramatic, erotic, perfect performance model for young, attractive couples. This is intimidating for older couples, especially those dealing with illness and disability. The performance model devalues mainstream couples—the message is your sexuality is not "good enough". GES is a motivating, empowering model for the great majority of couples. A major understanding is that couple sexuality is variable and flexible. This is the opposite of the media depiction of romantic love/passionate sex which is always functional, intense, and wonderful.

Another advantage of GES is acceptance of both synchronous and asynchronous sexual experiences. The majority of sexual encounters are asynchronous—positive for both partners, but better for one than the other. Accept the value of asynchronous sexuality. Everyone agrees that the best sex is synchronous (high levels of desire/pleasure/eroticism/satisfaction). Accepting asynchronous sexuality is empowering and becomes more important with aging. A challenging awareness is that, with aging, female sexual response is often easier and more reliable than male response. With young couples, asynchronous sex was better for the man. This often reverses with aging. Asynchronous sexuality is another example of the need to embrace variable, flexible couple sexuality with aging.

Gendered Challenges in Implementing GES

GES was originally developed for men dealing with erectile dysfunction (ED). GES is much easier for women to accept than men. Whether discussing desire or orgasm, GES is congruent with female sexuality. Female desire and orgasm are variable and flexible, not totally predictable nor autonomous. Your sexual experience is compatible with GES.

The core issue is responsive sexual desire. The 1–2 combination is being responsible for your desire and being an intimate sexual team. His desire to be sexual with you reinforces your desire and desirability. This contrasts with young adult sexual experiences when desire was not for who you are but his desire for sex. Women note that past experiences felt transactional, you could have been anyone. With aging you feel desired for yourself, especially that he needs your sexual interest and involvement to enhance his sexual desire and response. In your 20s and 30s he didn't need you to be sexually responsive. Aging facilitates genuine and human sexuality. Your desire is enhanced when you recognize that he values your touch. Sex is intimate and interactive, not autonomous or transactional. Your active involvement is very different than the "going along for the ride" experiences of years ago.

In scenarios where you pleasure him to orgasm, you know he values your touch. Just as important when he pleasures you to orgasm, you feel his genuine interest in your body and responsivity. This is not a mechanical sexual servicing. GES promotes genuine sexual experiences. Sexuality is an integrated couple experience of intimacy, pleasuring, and eroticism.

Why is GES such a challenge for men generally and aging men specifically? There are myriad challenges, but the simple answer is it is so different than how you learned about sex. The double standard is based on the mistaken assumption that male sexuality is superior. GES challenges those assumptions and invites you to embrace pleasure with your partner rather than perform for her. This reinforces the female–male sexual equity model which is much healthier than the double standard.

A crucial concept is accepting "responsive male sexual desire". This challenges the beliefs that spontaneous erection is the cue for desire, that male sexuality is superior, and that spontaneous desire is better than responsive desire. Openness to responsive desire promotes male, female, and couple desire with aging. It is normal and healthy to begin a sexual encounter at 0 (on a 10-point scale of subjective arousal). As you experience giving and receiving sensual and playful touching this elicits subjective pleasure/arousal of 2, 3 or 4. That is when you experience desire. You don't need an erection or "horny" feelings in order to engage sexually. Be open to pleasure-oriented touching to promote sexual receptivity and responsivity. GES is based on intimate, interactive sexuality rather than autonomous sex performance. You value your partner as your intimate and erotic ally.

You need her support to embrace GES. You will not get support from male friends, male doctors, drug companies, or the media. That is sad but true. The drug companies and culture tell you to look to external resources to build sex desire and function—pills, testosterone, a new diet, a powerful workout regimen, or whatever promotes your sense of masculinity (feeling powerful and in control). In contrast, GES is based on acceptance, turning toward your partner as your intimate and erotic ally, a pleasure orientation, and accepting variability and flexibility of couple sexuality. This is a complex, healthy, nuanced approach to masculinity.

Both men and women benefit from GES, but men benefit more. GES gives you freedom and options to enjoy sexuality that includes but is not limited to intercourse. The traditional male model emphasized "intercourse or nothing". Rather than deal with frustration and embarrassment you chose avoidance. You say to yourself, "I don't want to start something I can't finish". You reject GES concepts of responsive sexual desire and valuing sensual, playful, and erotic scenarios. You are stuck in "sex = intercourse". If you don't achieve intercourse you feel like a failure. You are trapped in the traditional male role.

GES is a new, healthy model for male (and couple) sexuality. GES promotes a genuine and humanistic approach to sexuality. A key is acceptance of the multiple roles, meanings, and outcomes of sexuality.

The ideal is a shared experience of desire/pleasure/eroticism/satisfaction which energizes your bond. Other roles include sex as a tension reducer, sex as fun and play, sex to reconnect after a conflict, sex to reinforce intimacy, one-way sex as an erotic experience, sex as a gift, sex to deal with boredom, sex as a port in the storm, sex for rebonding. In terms of meanings, sex can reinforce intimacy, lead to secure attachment, reinforce life meaning, sex as a playful connection, sex as a way to affirm life after the death of a sibling, sex as a means to feel together after launching a child into college, sex to recover after an argument, feel revitalized after a job loss, after the birth of a grandchild to reinforce feelings of being a family. In terms of outcomes, the ideal scenario is a mutual, synchronous, vital, and satisfying experience. Outcomes include sex as an asynchronous experience which was great for one partner and good for the other, sex which was routine but worthwhile, sex as erotically fulfilling for one partner and an intimate connection for the other, sex which was dysfunctional for one or both partners, sex which was fine for one partner but dissatisfying for the other, sex as a bonding experience. The message of GES is that sexuality is a couple experience with a range of roles, meanings, and outcomes. Couple sexuality is valued whether it was wonderful or dysfunctional. What is not healthy is sexual avoidance or sex as manipulation.

Sally and Seth

Sally, 79, and Seth, 82, had been a couple for over 60 years and a sexual couple for 56 years. They met during Sally's first week of college and Seth's first week after transferring from a community junior college. In their generation, couples would date and "make out" for months and years before beginning intercourse. Sally and Seth had memories of pleasurable touching and high desire. Sally had been the "gatekeeper" to ensure they did not proceed to intercourse. Seth remembers being frustrated but enjoying orgasm with Sally's manual stimulation or his rubbing against her. Although Sally enjoyed giving and receiving touching, she monitored her sexual response. She enjoyed manual breast stimulation but did not accept oral breast stimulation. Sally enjoyed the touching but was not orgasmic. Although sexuality was not equitable, she had very good memories of that time.

A contentious issue was when to begin intercourse. Five months before marrying, Seth's level of satisfaction dramatically increased when Sally agreed to intercourse. However, this was not true for Sally. She felt more like an adult woman, but sexual satisfaction decreased rather than increased. She did not voice her concerns. They fell into a sexual routine where all touching resulted in intercourse. If it did not Seth was irritated. Sally felt that sex was in Seth's control with an intercourse mandate. They no longer enjoyed sexual touching as a shared domain.

Sally and Seth had a traditional life organization focused on their three children, home, and Seth's career. This was typical for their generation. Their sexual relationship also followed the norm for their generation. Sex, especially intercourse initiation and frequency, was Seth's domain. Sally saw herself as a pro-sexual woman who was orgasmic during about a third of sexual encounters. Sex was better when the children were out of the house and best on their couple vacation when her parents watched the children. Seth and Sally seldom spoke about sexual issues. Their focus was on children, home, extended family, and Seth's career.

Sex was more important and satisfying for Seth. Most of their experiences were asynchronous, yet Sally felt accepting of their sexual relationship. As children became older, Sally felt overwhelmed by responsibilities, including a training program so she could rebuild her career. Sally attended an intensive week training. She appreciated Seth's emotional support, although she wished he would have changed his work schedule so he could provide practical support.

Balancing family, work, house, and friendships was challenging. Sally took their relationship for granted. Although somewhat disappointed, she accepted her life and marriage for what it was. This changed when Sally discovered that over three years, Seth had engaged in four "high opportunity/low involvement" affairs lasting between three weeks and four months. When discovered, Seth minimized the affairs as unimportant dalliances. Sally felt emotionally betrayed and did not accept the "boys will be boys" explanation. A counter-productive argument occurred when Seth said they didn't have a specific agreement about affairs, while Sally felt they had a firm agreement about no sex outside the marriage. Seth (the "involved" partner) and Sally (the "injured" partner) had totally different languages and understandings. They dealt with the affairs in a typical, unhealthy manner. Most marriages survive affairs—the easiest type to survive is the man's high opportunity/low involvement affair. Sadly, surviving is not the same as processing an affair, much less thriving after an affair. In retrospect, both Sally and Seth wish they had seen a couple therapist and processed the meaning of the affairs with a focus on intimacy and sexuality issues. What they did instead was have three meetings with their minister who stressed forgiveness and

God's support for their marriage and family, ignoring sexual issues. Seth said he was sorry and would respect their monogamy agreement in the future. This was not a bad outcome, but they would have benefitted from a therapeutic approach to make meaning of the affairs, build a strong trust bond, develop a couple sexual style, and create an individualized relapse prevention plan (McCarthy & Wald, 2013). Instead, their sexual relationship returned to the old pattern, but with less vitality and satisfaction, especially for Sally. They did not use the affair as an opportunity for growth. With affairs you cannot have a "do over". You can learn from the affair and use this to build a more meaningful, healthier couple sexuality. What happened with Seth and Sally was a continuation of the status quo for the next ten years.

The "empty nest" syndrome is a misnomer for most couples. With no children at home, the "couple again" phase is an opportunity to promote relational and sexual satisfaction. Sally and Seth had the time and energy to reexamine and revitalize their marriage and marital sexuality. Sally suggested they do what they should have done ten years earlier—see a couple therapist with a specialty in sexuality problems. The first meeting was as a couple to reinforce that intimacy and sexuality is a couple issue. The therapist was clear that they could not change the past, including the missed opportunity to process the affairs at the time. Power for change is in the present. They could process and learn from their experiences, including making genuine meaning of the affairs. In her individual session, Sally did not want to blame or shame Seth. She was puzzled how their sexual relationship had gotten so far off track. Specifically, how Sally lost her "sexual voice" (McCarthy & McCarthy, 2018). When discussing her perceptions about Seth's affairs, what became clear was her resentment that Seth had not "owned" the affairs nor processed his motivations. In his individual session, Seth admitted he had not examined his sexual motivations and not realized the depth of the emotional pain he had caused. Seth did not understand Sally's approach to sexuality and regretted that they had not explored this. Seth feared being labeled the "bad guy". He worried that the legacy of the affairs would define their marriage. He had chosen to avoid and downplay this issue.

The clinician started the 90-minute couple feedback session by congratulating them on having the courage to come to therapy and willingness to explore sexual problems. It was not a matter of blame or shame; it was acceptance of psychological strengths and vulnerabilities and building a new couple sexual style which would serve them for the next 30 years. A core concept is that "living well" relationally and sexually was in their control.

A key was Seth recognizing that the traditional double standard had been a mistake for him, Sally, their marriage, and couple sexuality. Seth took for granted totally predictable, autonomous sex function. He had not needed anything sexually from either Sally or the affair partners. Even through the drama of the affair discovery, Seth functioned autonomously. This reinforced his feeling of sexual control and made it harder to be emotionally vulnerable with Sally. Seth was willing to engage in couple therapy while his sexual function was easy. GES was not initially accepted by Seth although it was motivating for Sally. Ultimately, GES became a crucial component in their new couple sexual style.

In making genuine meaning of the affairs, Seth had to confront his belief that he was sexually superior to Sally. This was a major cause of his inability to process the affairs and its impact on their relationship. More important, it blocked them from creating a new couple sexuality as part of the healing process.

Ideally, couples adopt GES before there is a crisis. Seth prided himself on being pro-sexual, but his definition of sex was narrow, focused on spontaneous erection and intercourse. Seth saw himself as always ready to go and Sally had to be stimulated so she could catch up. "Foreplay" was for Sally, intercourse for Seth. Could Seth learn to value sensual, playful, and erotic scenarios for himself and them as a couple? Could Seth accept that Sally's intimacy and eroticism needs were as important as his? Could he recognize that a genuine apology, not just for the affairs but for his demanding approach to intercourse, would free Sally to be an equitable sexual partner? This meant Seth giving up traditional male sex privilege. A benefit of female–male sexual equity is they would be intimate and erotic friends. Seth valuing predictable erections and intercourse was fine with Sally. What she needed from Seth was affirmation that her variable, flexible sexual response was healthy and that sexuality was more than intercourse. In therapy Seth and Sally confronted their sexual histories. More important they developed a Complementary couple sexual style which honored each person's sexual voice while being an intimate sexual team. Sally found GES congruent with her lived sexual experiences and promoted a new vital, satisfying couple sexuality.

Now, 30 years later they are enjoying the sexuality with aging life phase. Sally and Seth were pleased that they had invested nine months in couple therapy. Sally used the analogy that it took the full nine months to give birth to a new couple sexuality. GES expectations and experiences served them well with aging. As a sexually satisfied 82-year-old man, Seth is grateful that he adopted GES before there was a sex dysfunction problem. Seth preferred intercourse but was open to playful and erotic scenarios, both synchronous and asynchronous. Sally had a strong preference for synchronous erotic sexuality. She was pleased Seth piggybacked his arousal on hers. Sexuality was more satisfying for her than at any time in the marriage. When they look back at how sex had gotten off track, they feel regretful, but not blaming. They value couple sexuality with aging.

GES in Context

GES was originally developed with men suffering from sex dysfunction, especially ED. Interestingly, GES has been more accepted by women than men. Unfortunately, this is also true for aging men. This is sad because GES is a particularly good fit for aging men and couples. A key strength is recognizing that the essence of sexuality is sharing pleasure. Another empowering concept is accepting the multiple roles, meanings, and outcomes of sexuality. Sexuality is variable and flexible, not a simplistic performance test. GES is a good fit for the man, woman, couple, and culture. Embracing GES is a challenge because it does not fit the media ideal of a couple in great health, physically fit, enjoying dramatic and flawless sex. The way sex is depicted in the media is intimidating—the message is "you are not good enough". This is a frustrating conundrum for older couples.

GES is much easier to accept in a couple context. Marketing people say "Good Enough Sex" is not a saleable title. Drug company people say what wins men over are promises of "cure" and being "powerful". Intimacy-based couple therapists emphasize love and security, not sexuality. GES speaks to the reality of most peoples' sexual experiences—sometimes special, usually good although better for one partner, sometimes okay, and on occasion disappointing or dysfunctional. Can you accept the range of sexual roles, meanings, and outcomes? Can you celebrate special sexual experiences as well as okay ones? The attitude of acceptance is crucial. Some aging couples have a wonderful experience in 90% of encounters. Count yourselves lucky. For most couples, variability of sexual outcomes is the norm. The test of couple sexuality is to turn toward each other when the experience is mediocre or dysfunctional for one or both partners. No apologizing or panicking. Sexual acceptance is the crucial message.

Exercise: Implementing GES

This exercise asks you to purposefully engage in four different scenarios—sensual, playful, erotic, and intercourse. The challenge is to determine whether each dimension (gear) is positive for you. Ideally, couples are comfortable with all four scenarios. It is common that you agree to drop one or even two scenarios. It is crucial to have at least three touching dimensions (gears). Most common are affection, erotic, and intercourse. Some couples drop the erotic dimension, others the playful dimension, and still others the sensual dimension. The important factor is what dimensions of GES are integrated in your relationship. We suggest an open, exploratory approach, focusing on one scenario at a time. For example, the playful scenario involves both genital and non-genital pleasuring, enjoying 4–5 subjective arousal.

The erotic scenario involves sensations/feelings in the 6–10 range and can include manual, oral, rubbing, or vibrator stimulation. Experiment with mutual, synchronous, or one-way erotic scenarios. What is the right fit for you? Does erotic sexuality involving orgasm fit?

Explore the sensual dimension with subjective arousal in the 1–3 range. Sensual sexuality is a solid base for your relationship. Many find it more enjoyable for the woman than the man. Does sensuality fit your GES experience? This exercise is to make personal and concrete that sensual, playful, and erotic scenarios are sexual and integral to GES.

The second part of this exercise is to accept GES whether the experience was wonderful or dissatisfying. It is almost impossible to plan a dissatisfying or dysfunctional sexual experience. In the next two months when you experience dissatisfying or dysfunctional sex do you turn to your partner with a sense of acceptance? Acceptance and remaining on the same sexual team is a core component of GES. You don't want a negative sexual encounter, but dissatisfying or dysfunctional experiences are part of normal couple sexuality. Rather than blaming or feeling embarrassed, the measure of a healthy couple is acceptance of the experience. Whether it was negative for one or both partners, accept the experience as a sexual team. This will not sell as a movie or novel, but is the reality for the great majority of couples. Being able to play this out at least once builds individual and relational confidence. Any couple can enjoy sex if everything goes well. The challenge is to be intimate and erotic allies when sex is mediocre, dissatisfying, or dysfunctional. Reading and talking about GES is valuable, but the real value is implementing and experiencing these concepts.

As with any exercise, practice and feedback are crucial. This is especially true in implementing GES expectations and accepting the range of GES outcomes.

Summary

Although GES was not developed for aging couples, it is most valuable with aging. GES is a key strategy to celebrate sexuality and aging. Clinging to intercourse as a pass–fail sex test leads to frustration, embarrassment, and eventually avoidance. GES immunizes you against these common traps. The core concept is that sexuality is a more genuine couple experience with aging. This confronts the individual performance model. Embrace sensual, playful, and erotic scenarios as integral to your sexuality.

The 85% guideline of touching leading to intercourse becomes more variable with aging. For some couples it is 75%, others 33%, and still others 10%. Intercourse is valued but no longer the dominant factor. If intercourse is not part of your sexual repertoire, embrace a variable, flexible approach to erotic sexuality.

A critical component of GES is focusing on couple sexuality more than individual sex. Enjoy the multiple roles and meanings of sexuality. By its nature, couple sexuality is variable and flexible. The best sexual experiences are mutual and synchronous, although most sex is positive but asynchronous. Asynchronous sexuality becomes more common with aging. Aging couples accept and celebrate complex, multi-dimensional sexual experiences. Value sexuality with illness and disability. A prime strength of GES is acceptance of couple sexuality with its diverse roles, meanings, and outcomes. Acceptance facilitates sexual expression into your 80s.

5

FEMALE–MALE SEXUAL EQUITY: BEING INTIMATE AND EROTIC FRIENDS

The traditional double standard splits intimacy (for women) and eroticism (for men) resulting in a sexual power struggle. In contrast, the female–male sexual equity model emphasizes both partners valuing intimacy and eroticism. The sexual equity model recognizes there are many more sexual similarities than differences between men and women (Hyde, 2005). This is especially true for couples over 60. Both genders affirm that pleasure is the foundation for sexuality and aging.

Ideally, couples adopt the female–male sexual equity model in their 20s, but that is not the reality (especially not for the present generation of older adults). The double standard was the norm in your generation. The culture and media treated male–female differences as natural and unchangeable. The assumption was that men were stronger and more sexual. Female sexuality was dependent on relational factors and burdened by fear of negative consequences and stigma. The double standard is scientifically wrong. Its narrow constraints are harmful, but it was easy to learn and was reinforced by cultural and family norms.

An advantage of aging is greater awareness and choice. You value flexibility in gender roles and make "wise" decisions. One of the wisest decisions is to adopt the female–male equity model, especially sexual equity. This entails more than socially desirable words, it is a psychological, relational, and sexual commitment to being a healthy couple. You approach each other as respectful, trusting, emotional friends. You feel loved for who you are, not based on narrow gender stereotypes. You cannot change mistakes from the past, but you can learn from them.

Make wise relational and sexual decisions. Be intimate and erotic friends as you deal with your own and your partner's aging. The best example of being sexual friends is being open to your partner's influence. In the double standard the woman begged or manipulated while the man asserted his rights as "head of the family". You complained to same gender friends and made fun of the opposite sex. Women "put up" with the man and his sexual pushiness since men were expected to push sex. It sounds so silly and dated, but these over-learned, self-defeating patterns burden your relationship. The challenge is to change how you relate and to promote a positive influence process. Be receptive and responsive to touch. As intimate and erotic partners you accept both synchronous and asynchronous sexual experiences. Adopt the desire/pleasure/eroticism/satisfaction mantra. This is quite different than the double standard sexual routine. The traditional script involved you having a spontaneous erection, performing "foreplay" where you stimulated her (she was passive) until you felt she was ready for intercourse, inserted your penis, and set the rhythm of intercourse thrusting. Your orgasm ended the sexual encounter (you asked whether she had an orgasm). Sometimes you had minimally involving afterplay consisting of a kiss and saying, "I love you". This was a highly predictable scenario based on your sexual script and preferences.

At the beginning of your sexual relationship (limerence phase) sex was engaging for the woman, but over time you lost your sexual voice and gave in to routine, mediocre sex. This resulted in secondary low desire which affects one in three women. This sexual pattern went on for years or even decades. The usual struggle was you wanted more intimacy and he wanted more intercourse. You were speaking a different sexual language in an adversarial, blaming manner. This self-defeating power struggle needs to be confronted. It is the opposite of being intimate and erotic allies.

Female–Male Sexual Equity

The optimal strategy is to build a new model of female–male sexual equity. The core of this model is awareness that there are more sexual similarities than differences between men and women. This is even more true with aging. A healthy sexual relationship involves two fully functioning individuals. Honor differences, whether based on psychological, biomedical, or social/relational factors, while reinforcing similarities. Ideally, both partners value desire/pleasure/eroticism/satisfaction and the 15–20% role of sexuality. Ensure that sexual conflicts or problems do not undermine your relationship. Be intimate and erotic allies who experience sex as energizing and reinforce feelings of desire and desirability. The sexual equity model is compatible with the Good Enough Sex (GES) model and reinforces positive, realistic expectations of sexuality with aging. You cannot compare aging sexuality with the limerence phase of a youthful, idealized relationship. An advantage is feeling genuinely bonded and energized in your 60s, 70s, and 80s. Turn toward each other whether the sexual encounter was wonderful or dysfunctional. Do not just say the words, emotionally accept your sexual experiences. Acceptance is the foundation for sexuality with aging. From this foundation you can explore and experiment. You have freedom to be who you are as aging partners. The sexual equity model gives you options which are not possible in the double standard. The equity model frees men to adopt variable, flexible sexual expression rather than limit sex to intercourse. It allows women to celebrate sensual, playful, and erotic sexuality. This validates a broad, flexible approach to intimacy and sexuality. You are not a second-class person who has to be sexual within the rules of the traditional male model. He needs you to be sexually responsive in a manner he didn't 20 years ago. Aging sexuality embraces equity as good for the woman, man, couple, and culture. A downside is regret and resentment that you did not adopt the equity model earlier, but it is not too late. It is hard to see any advantage of the double standard with aging. People cling to the double standard because you are used to it. Couples say, "Why change if it's not broken?". The truth is the double standard has been broken for years, often decades. Ideally, you adopt the equity model in your 20s or 30s, but it is never too late. Embracing sexual equity is one of your wisest decisions.

Relational Equity and Sexual Equity

Relational equity and sexual equity are different but complementary. There is more cultural support for relational than sexual equity. We advocate a "both-and" approach. Relational equity need not occur first. In Barry's clinical practice, couples found that sexual growth promoted relational equity. Intimacy and eroticism promote respect and trust.

The traditional gender split pits emotional vs. sexual intimacy, leading to a power struggle. Intimacy promotes a positive influence process which results in enhanced relational and sexual health. Ideally, you implement relational and sexual equity in tandem. The equity model reinforces respect, trust, and emotional closeness. Respecting yourself and your partner is the core of relational equity. Whether discussing work, finances, parenting, or household tasks, strive to be a team. Do not try to split everything 50–50. In dividing domains be aware of your preferences and skills. A functional, satisfying system is more important than a "socially desirable" 50–50 system. Each person uniquely contributes to your relationship. Your contributions are acknowledged and appreciated. Recognize that there are times when one spouse "carries" the relationship. Acknowledge this rather than foster resentment. You are not clones of each other in terms of interests, skills, and energy.

In the past you fell into traditional gender complaints and put-downs. When reviewing your relational history be cognizant of the importance of processing past issues. This is therapeutic as opposed to the blaming/retribution approach. Processing and awareness motivate you to be healthy partners in the present. In contrast, blaming, shaming, and retribution keep you stuck in the past and negate equity. Focus on promoting relational well-being. Only 30% of relational problems are resolvable, 50–60% are modifiable, and even in the healthiest relationships 10–20% of problems need to be accepted and worked around (Gottman & Silver, 2015). Positive, realistic expectations are crucial in an equitable relationship. Unfortunately, many couples emphasize stability rather than promote relational satisfaction. Healthy marriages are satisfying, secure, and sexual. Perfectionistic expectations undercut relational satisfaction. Positive, realistic expectations support equity and satisfaction. Rather than a gender split, both partners affirm the importance of a satisfying relationship and satisfying sexuality. The traditional split built antagonism and resentment, the equity model reinforces a genuine, satisfying relationship.

Female–male equity emphasizes both partners valuing a secure bond, rather than just a stable marriage. Stable ensures you will remain a couple, secure means you value your spouse and relationship. A secure relationship promotes equity. Sadly, a stable relationship often results in a disappointing and frustrating marriage. Being in a healthy marriage brings out healthy parts of each person. Settling for a stable relationship undercuts individual well-being and relational satisfaction.

The "common sense" approach emphasized that love and communication was all that was needed. Aging couples realize that is misleading at best, and often harmful. We are in favor of love and communication, but that is not enough. Traditional approaches do not include loving the partner with their vulnerabilities and dealing with unresolvable problems. The love and communication model does not accept that only 30% of relational problems are resolvable. The mistaken assumption is that with love and communication everything is resolvable. This sets you up for hurt and disappointment. The equity model encourages love and communication, but not as the answer to all problems. We encourage emotional problem-solving. You can learn from the past, but do not litigate the past. You are emotional friends and are open to your spouse's positive influence.

Female–Male Sexual Equity

Sexuality has a paradoxical role in your lives, especially with aging. Sexuality energizes your bond and reinforces feelings of desire and desirability. When couples cease sex it has an inordinately negative impact—demoralizing you and draining your bond of intimacy. Older couples are unlikely to divorce. However, being a non-sexual couple results in an emotional and sexual stalemate. Although you seldom talk about it, there is blame and counter blame about the loss of intimacy and sexuality. Even couples with chronic sex dysfunction miss an intimate attachment. Your marriage is stable, but marginal. The contrast with couples who value sexual equity is striking. You celebrate affection, sensual, playful, and erotic touching both outside and inside the bedroom. Sexual equity promotes attachment and pleasure even when intercourse frequency and function is lessened. Barry remembers a couple who prided themselves in being sexual three to four times a week throughout their marriage. Now in their 70s they enjoy an erotic or intercourse encounter at least once a week. In addition, they value sensual and playful touching. He particularly enjoys being playful in front of the fireplace while watching a Masterpiece Theatre video. She values mutual erotic scenarios in the children's old bedrooms. They have pleasant memories, but feel that couple sexuality is the most satisfying in the present.

The equity model reinforces the value of your relationship, especially turning toward each other when life is frustrating or stressful. A famous saying is, "I trust my spouse has my back" (Johnson, 2008). Your spouse may not agree with you about an issue, but you are confident he would not do anything to intentionally hurt or undercut you. At times you feel disappointed, hurt, or angry. That is normal in an intimate relationship. The old view, "Love means never having to say you're sorry", is emotionally seductive but untrue. You say you're sorry at least once a month. The essence of trust is you believe your spouse cares about you and would not intentionally do something to hurt you.

The role of sexuality is to energize your bond. Most couples have an emotional commitment (monogamy) to not be sexual with others. You are affectionate with friends or family, but refrain from sexual touching. You care about your spouse and their feelings. That is why it is such a loss when couples stop sex. It is not just ceasing intercourse; you stop sensual and playful touch. This leaves a large void. Sensual, playful, and erotic touch affirms the value of your relationship. Touching adds vitality to your bond.

Each partner has sexual strengths and vulnerabilities. A major concept is to affirm female sexuality as first class, not inferior to male sexuality. Female sexuality is more variable, flexible, and individualistic, yet first class. With aging, sexual similarities increase but, sadly, gender vulnerabilities become more apparent. The male vulnerability is the narrow definition of sex as intercourse, overemphasizing control and performance. This results in sexual avoidance because you cannot live up to perfectionistic performance demands. The female vulnerability is to negate your sexual feelings and preferences, viewing sex as his domain. You lose your sexual voice. In the equity model you accept each other's preferences for intimacy, pleasuring, and eroticism. Sexuality brings out the best in each person and you as a couple. Sexuality becomes more human and genuine with aging. Being emotional and sexual friends reinforces being an intimate team.

Rachel and Doug

81-year-old Rachel had been divorced and later widowed in a second marriage. She married 74-year-old Doug six years ago. They began their marriage committed to the female–male equity model.

Doug was divorced when he was 58. He was devastated when his marriage ended. The ex-wife told Doug he was a bad person, especially insisting on being sexually dominant and demanding intercourse. Doug thought he would enjoy being single with a choice of women, but found the singles scene alienating and disappointing. There was too much emotional drama and alcohol abuse. As he aged, Doug found alcohol inhibited sexual response. Even more, alcohol brought out emotional antagonism. Whether the woman was his age or younger, the level of drama overwhelmed Doug. He decided not to be involved with women younger than 50 because he did not trust their motivations.

Rachel and Doug met through mutual friends. They were open to a relationship, although neither expected to remarry. Doug was impressed by Rachel's assertiveness, especially her right to be treated as a first-class woman emotionally and sexually. She let him know she had herpes, although outbreaks were rare. She insisted they go together to take an HIV test and STI screen so they could take reasonable measures to be sexually safe. Rachel said if they were to be a serious couple, she would not tolerate him being sexual with other women, especially his ex-wife. Doug was embarrassed to admit that since the divorce he had sex one to three times a year with his ex-wife. Alcohol abuse, negative emotions, and dramatic sex were followed by weeks of conflict and recriminations. In contrast, Rachel affirmed Doug as an intimate partner. Doug was pleased that over months their relationship became more satisfying. They maintained separate residences, but spent increasing time together.

Rachel believes a woman is healthier when she maintains her own identity and autonomy. Rachel was a dedicated volunteer at a modern art museum and took the commitment seriously. Doug learned to schedule couple activities on non-museum days.

Both valued intimacy, pleasuring, and eroticism. Doug was proud of his emotional and sexual growth. Sexual quality was more important than quantity. Sometimes sex was intimate, sometimes playful, sometimes erotic, and sometimes sharing warm feelings. Doug looked back on his sexual past with regret. His ex-wife was right that he had been demanding and intercourse focused. Sexuality with Rachel was flexible and pleasurable, a shared domain. As months turned to years their relationship thrived. One night Doug made reservations at an upscale restaurant and after dessert presented Rachel with a beautiful bracelet and asked her to marry him. This was totally unexpected. Rachel was reluctant to risk a third marriage and felt uneasy about their age difference as well as family and financial issues. There were a number of potential problems, but their commitment to the equity model made it easier to dialogue about these issues. Their adult children were not in favor of the marriage although all three of their grandchildren were supportive. The sexual equity model energized them and provided motivation to deal with housing, financial, and family decisions. The equity model recognizes that there are few perfect resolutions, but you can reach agreements that work. For example, Rachel loved her three-story house, but realized as she aged that a single-story home made more sense. Doug suggested buying a single-story home that was large enough to accommodate the antique furniture Rachel was fond of. In addition to a well-designed master bedroom there was a second bedroom and bathroom for visiting family and friends. Doug used his financial resources to build a fireplace in the master bedroom which became their favorite setting for sex.

Older couples have successful second marriages because they do not fall into a relationship driven by idealistic love and dramatic sex. Each person has a clear view of self as well as the strengths and vulnerabilities of the perspective spouse. This makes them more likely to make wise decisions. Doug and Rachel put time and energy into developing a satisfying, secure, and sexual marriage. Doug made it clear that if Rachel was upset about his behavior she needed to tell him. He wanted to know rather than let things build and have a blow-up. He wanted to be aware and not take their relationship for granted. Rachel valued emotional and sexual intimacy. She was appreciative that Doug valued affectionate, sensual, erotic, and intercourse touch. Rachel did not enjoy playful touch and Doug accepted that.

An important couple activity was swimming laps. They tried to schedule swimming at least five times a week, with Doug usually doing five additional laps. They were sexual at least once a week—whether erotic or intercourse sex. Rachel was orgasmic before intercourse and Doug orgasmic during intercourse. Rachel valued sexual variability and flexibility. She enjoyed self-entrancement arousal more than Doug. He found her sexual responsivity highly erotic and enjoyed partner interaction arousal. As they aged sexuality remained validating. They did not engage in "what if" discussions about previous relationships. They valued their marriage. As an aging woman, Rachel found the equity bond was crucial. She felt attractive and valued. She enjoyed that Doug piggybacked his arousal on hers. The female–male equity model reinforced vitality and security.

Do Not Take Sexual Equity for Granted

Complacency is a danger for older couples. Sexual equity cannot be treated as a done deal. We have been married 54 years and do not take our sexuality for granted. Individually and as a couple commit to sexual equity. This is especially important as illness and side-effects of medications take more of a role in your lives. Rather than being afraid or withdrawn, turn toward your spouse. Sexuality is an ongoing process involving balancing the needs and preferences of both partners. This includes changes with aging, illness, disability, and medications. Awareness and dialogue are necessary. Balance your attitudes, behaviors, and emotions with being an intimate sexual team. Your partner's sexual preference cannot be at your expense. For example, one partner enjoyed receiving oral sex, but the spouse developed breathing problems which made giving oral sex uncomfortable and anxiety provoking. The receiving partner accepted the less erotic experience of manual stimulation. It was a powerful statement about the priority of sharing pleasure as an equitable team. When you get your way sexually at the expense of your partner you win the battle but lose the war for a satisfying sexual relationship. Winning a battle at the expense of your relationship is self-defeating. Sexual equity is based on a positive influence process. Asynchronous sexuality is not at the expense of your partner or relationship. Sexual equity recognizes that you are not clones of each other. Accepting differences and enjoying your partner's sexual preferences spices up your relationship. Differences promote vital, satisfying couple sexuality.

Exercise: Implementing the Female–Male Sexual Equity Model

Changing attitudes, feelings, and values is of great importance, but the real change occurs in implementing new behavior patterns. Good words and good intentions alone do not promote growth. You need to integrate this into your sexual relationship. Developing a new couple sexual style (likely the Complementary style) allows you to be intimate and erotic allies who enjoy sharing desire/pleasure/eroticism/satisfaction.

This exercise has three components. First, establish a sexual repertoire that respects each person's sexual voice and unique strengths. Second, implement changes in sexual initiation, pleasuring, eroticism, intercourse, and orgasm which is a good fit for each partner and your relationship. Third, recognize your sexual vulnerabilities and deal with these so they do not subvert sexual equity. Remember, the goal is not perfection, but equity. Each person is unique, not controlled by gender stereotypes. Be clear about each partner's sexual strengths and vulnerabilities.

Traditionally, men felt powerful, initiated sex with a spontaneous erection, easily felt erotic flow, went to intercourse on their first erection, and were orgasmic during intercourse. A strength of traditional male sex was control and predictability. Rather than trying to live up to these performance demands, what do you need in your new sexual repertoire to feel good about yourself as an aging sexual man? What are your unique strengths which reinforce your sexual voice? What allows you to feel like a first-class aging partner?

For women, a strength is appreciating your sexual voice and responsivity. Recognize sexual similarities but value the unique characteristics of your sexual voice. Women value variable, flexible sexuality, responsive sexual desire, acceptance of both synchronous and asynchronous sexual scenarios, and finding your erotic voice. In addition, accept your orgasmic pattern. Be aware of the range of roles, meanings, and outcomes of couple sexuality. Be clear and specific about being a first-class sexual woman with aging.

What does it mean to acknowledge each person's unique sexual voice? Do not go on to the second phase of this exercise until both partners see each other as a unique, first-class sexual person.

Explore sexual patterns that reinforce being an equitable sexual team. Do you have similar or unique bridges to sexual desire? Do you accept responsive sexual desire? Is sexual initiation a shared domain or is your partner more likely to initiate? Are your initiations unique or predictable? Is each partner free to veto a sexual scenario? How do you know if touching is for play or will lead to intercourse? Do you prefer to let sexual feelings simmer to enhance desire? Is a body massage likely to lead to intercourse? Do you have a favorite time to be sexual, a favorite room to be sexual, a favorite initiation scenario? Does your spouse accept your initiations and bridges to desire?

Can you change gender roles regarding intimacy and eroticism? You do not need a 50–50 split, but for both partners to value intimacy and eroticism. It is not unusual for one to prefer partner interaction arousal while the other prefers self-entrancement arousal. As long as it does not become a "right–wrong" power struggle this is normal and healthy. A power struggle where the man says, "Why can't you have orgasms like me?"—a single orgasm during intercourse—is destructive for the woman and couple. In the sexual equity model, you enjoy your orgasmic pattern (whether that is 70% of encounters using multiple stimulation during intercourse, an 80% orgasmic pattern with oral stimulation, or a 60% orgasm pattern during afterplay). He accepts your pattern rather than comparing it to his. Acceptance is the foundation of sexual equity. Openness to additions and changes empowers the equity model. What is not acceptable is the winner–loser approach. Sexual equity is the opposite of a zero-sum game.

Carefully review your initiation patterns, bridges to desire, non-demand pleasuring, playful touch, erotic scenarios, how you transition to intercourse, your intercourse preferences, and your orgasmic experience. Are you an equitable sexual team? What are up to three things you can change to promote sexual equity? Create a plan to implement these changes.

The third component of this exercise is the most challenging. What are personal and couple vulnerabilities that destabilize your equitable sexual bond? A major problem is when one spouse is not committed to the new model. Usually, but not always, it is the man. He is used to the prerogatives and privileges of the double standard. He wants sex to be better for you and is willing to help, but is not open to personal change. Or the woman feels sex is not an important part of your relationship—"It is what it is". You are not willing to put time, effort, and dialogue into creating an equitable sexual relationship. Often, it takes a sex dysfunction or a crisis to motivate change. That is sad because the change process is easier when there is a joint commitment to sexual growth.

A vulnerability is when one or both partners have a history of sexual trauma or are trying to protect a sexual secret. This makes sexuality a threatening topic. Many people have a "contingent sexual self-esteem", fearing that if the partner knew your sexual history, you would feel shameful and be rejected. In contrast, the sexual equity model encourages you to share sexual vulnerabilities and process painful experiences. You are a "proud survivor" not a "depressed, angry, or shameful victim". Living well is the best revenge (Maltz, 2012). Processing a vulnerability, whether with a therapist or your spouse, is crucial in your sexual healing journey. In Barry's clinical experience, a large number of men and women have been burdened for ten (or 50) years by their "shameful sexual secret". When disclosed, the spouse is usually accepting and supportive. Sexual secrets are more than a vulnerability. Sexual secrets poison your self-esteem and relationship. Confronting and processing sexual secrets and trauma is crucial.

Almost no individual or couple reach age 60 without at least one (usually many more) sexual experiences that cause guilt or regret. This is a vulnerability almost all of us share. You can learn from the past but cannot change the past. What you can do is confront and process secrets so they do not subvert sexual equity in the present.

Accepting personal and couple vulnerabilities as part of the human condition is therapeutic. No person and no relationship is perfect. A strength of the equity model is you feel accepted for who you are, with strengths and vulnerabilities.

This exercise motivates and empowers you to implement the female–male sexual equity model. In adopting the equity model you have freedom to enjoy sexuality with its range of roles, meanings, and outcomes.

Summary

The double standard has controlled the sexuality of men, women, and couples across generations and cultures. It is a simplistic model which subverts individual and couple sexuality. The harmfulness of the double standard becomes more evident with aging. Men stop sex because of frustration and embarrassment that they cannot live up to the sexual demands of the double standard. In contrast, the female–male equity model empowers you to value sexuality in your 60s, 70s, and 80s. Sexuality is more human and genuine, but also more challenging (especially for men). With freedom comes challenge. You are intimate and erotic allies. Pleasure-oriented touching is the core of couple sexuality. Sexuality includes sensual, playful, and erotic scenarios in addition to intercourse. Penetration and intercourse no longer define sex. Sexuality involves desire/pleasure/eroticism/satisfaction and does not require intercourse. Sexuality is not an individual intercourse and orgasm test. Sexuality is a team sport. Partners turn toward each other as sexual friends. Enjoy freedom you never could with the double standard. You cling to the double standard because that is what you know. Men do not discuss sexual equity with male peers. Women often advocate for equity with their friends. You have the power to advocate for sexual equity in your marriage. Female–male sexual equity brings out the best in women, men, couples, and the culture.

6

DESIRE IS THE KEY: REINFORCING SEXUAL ANTICIPATION

Desire is the core dimension for sexuality and aging. In contrast to the male model of spontaneous desire (illustrated by his erection) this new awareness reinforces the superiority of "responsive sexual desire". Responsive desire is relevant for both men and women, although originally developed for women (Basson, 2007). In the mantra of desire/pleasure/eroticism/satisfaction, desire is the most important dimension. The core of responsive desire is awareness and receptivity to touching. When you are emotionally and physically receptive to touch and feel subjective arousal, that is when you experience desire and willingness to engage in a sexual encounter. Emotional and physical responsivity elicits sexual desire rather than hoping for or demanding spontaneous desire.

There are myriad factors which facilitate desire and myriad factors which can subvert desire. These include psychological, biomedical, and social/relational factors. Let's start with psychological factors. First is positive anticipation. In the same manner that you look forward to attending your favorite athletic event, restaurant, or cultural offering, you anticipate touching and sexuality. Second is a sense of deserving pleasure at this point in your life and in this relationship. Pleasure is not contingent on beauty, perfect performance, or anything else. You deserve pleasure even when you are dealing with cancer, your adult children are not thriving, your house has leaks, you or your spouse has a disability, you regret poor life choices, you need hearing aids. You deserve sexual pleasure as an aging person and couple. A third psychological factor is freedom and choice. This is grounded on your ability to say no to sex or a specific sexual scenario. Unless you have the power to say no, you don't have the freedom to say yes to sex. Freedom involves present sexual preferences and choices, not what elicited desire five or 40 years ago. You are free to embrace the flexibility and variability of aging sexuality. A final psychological factor is unpredictable sexual scenarios and techniques. It's normal for desire and arousal to wane, but it can wax again. Variability in sexual response allows you to create sexual alternatives. Sexuality is more human and genuine with aging. Couples, particularly men, value sexual predictability and control. Rather than mourn this loss with aging, we encourage you to embrace the challenge of less predictable sexual scenarios, enjoy exploration, and take sexual risks. Accept that not all sex will be good—some encounters will be exceptional, others dissatisfying. A challenge is to accept (and enjoy) a variety of sexual roles, meanings, and outcomes.

We emphasize building sexual desire, but it is equally important to be aware of what subverts desire. A major factor is performance as well as anticipatory anxiety. When you approach sex as an individual pass–fail performance test you are on the road to low desire. It's not just subverting the pleasure orientation, you are not an intimate sexual team. You are performing for your partner rather than sharing with her. Performance is about proving something to yourself or your partner. This burdens desire. Another factor interfering with desire is anger, whether about sexual or relational, past or present issues. People have angry sex, but in the long run anger inhibits desire. Another major factor is losing your sexual voice. Sex is to placate your partner, not sex for you and your relationship.

People are surprised to learn that when couples become non-sexual (sex less than ten times a year), it is almost always the man's choice (McKinlay & Feldman, 1994). He makes it unilaterally and conveys it non-verbally. It is not that he wants to stop sex, but he has lost confidence with erection and intercourse. For him, sex is a frustrating and embarrassing performance failure. To make it worse, he blames the sexual problems on his spouse (or on children, money, politics, the world). Rather than sex being energizing, it causes isolation and alienation. Another negative factor is a sexual secret such as a variant arousal pattern which is highly erotically charged but negates couple sex. Or the secret involves shame over a sexual orientation conflict or a history of sexual trauma. Psychologically, desire is amazingly easy to kill.

There is a different pattern for female low desire. A major factor is you have lost your sexual voice. Unlike previous generations where women did not value sexual pleasure, you discovered the joy of sex. You valued desire, pleasure, and orgasm. However, after sex fell into the routine of the man initiating, performing foreplay to get you ready for intercourse, and controlling intercourse thrusting, sex became an uninviting routine. It reinforced your feeling that sex was his domain, not yours nor was it a shared domain. Secondary low desire is the most common female sex dysfunction, impacting one in three adult women (Brotto & Velten, 2020).

Let us explore biomedical factors that enhance desire. The news is good. There is clear scientific evidence that you can be sexual until age 85 (Lindau et al., 2007). We believe you can be sexual after 85 if you accept the new normal of your body and focus on a broad, flexible approach to sexual touching. A crucial biomedical concept is that anything which is good for your physical body is good for your sexuality. It is not aging which interferes with sexuality, especially not desire. Being healthy and fit promotes sexual health. Especially important are good sleeping patterns. In addition, exercise, healthy eating, no smoking, and moderate or no drinking are good for your physical and sexual health.

Another important concept is there is no illness or disability which stops sexual desire. Medical problems change sexual function, but do not destroy desire. A key to desire is your accepting the new normal.

If you have an illness or disability, a specific suggestion is to schedule a couple consultation with your primary care doctor or specialist (cardiologist for heart and blood pressure, endocrinologist for diabetes or hormonal problems, psychiatrist for depression or anxiety, a pain specialist). Most physicians are not well trained on sexual issues (especially sexuality and aging). However, physicians want to be helpful. If you consult the physician as a couple it brings out the best in the doctor. Physicians are used to seeing patients individually and dealing with biomedical problems. Seeing you as a couple and discussing sexuality and aging broadens the framework and allows the physician to provide biomedical information and engage in problem-solving. A common cause of sexual problems is side-effects of medications. The physician can prescribe a medication with fewer sexual side-effects, change medication dosage, or alter when you take the medication.

One of the best ways to get a man to stop smoking is to tell him that smoking is bad for his penis (or for the woman's vulva). Smoking interferes with vascular function—impacting erections and vaginal lubrication. Another biomedical intervention is helping reduce pain (sexual and other pain) by consulting a physical therapist with a sexual pain specialty. You can learn mindfulness and relaxation techniques.

Rather than hoping a medication will function as a stand-alone intervention, biomedical interventions are most efficacious in the context of a comprehensive approach to understanding and changing psychological and relational factors.

The third domain is social/relational. A major challenge is to integrate intimacy and eroticism. Another challenge is to establish and maintain positive, realistic sexual expectations.

Contrary to the assumption of the public and of marriage therapists, a common cause of low desire is too much emphasis on intimacy and mutuality, causing you to de-eroticize each other and your relationship. Although intimacy and mutuality are good, too much can interfere with sexual desire. The challenge for older couples, married or partnered, straight or gay, is to integrate intimacy and eroticism. Different couple sexual styles promote different balances. Eroticism plays an integral role in desire for both women and men. Maintaining your erotic voice with aging is a critical challenge. Eroticism is not based on visual stimuli, but touch stimuli. This is especially true for partner interaction and self-entrancement arousal/eroticism. Both partners valuing intimacy and eroticism strengthens your sexual relationship.

Positive, Realistic Sexual Expectations

A major cause of desire problems is the romantic love/passionate sex/idealization model. In the media, sex is portrayed as dramatic and perfect—like an R-rated movie. In this image, sex is always mutual and synchronous. Enjoy the limerence phase of romantic love/passionate sex, but realize it is fragile and time-limited—usually 6–12 months, seldom two years. You need to transition from limerence to develop a couple sexual style with strong, resilient desire.

Positive, realistic sexual expectations are very important. The best sex is mutual and synchronous. Synchronous means both partners experience high levels of desire/pleasure/eroticism/satisfaction. Most sexual experiences are positive but asynchronous. Asynchronous means the sexual encounter was positive, but better for one partner. Asynchronous sex is healthy as long as it's not at the expense of the partner or relationship. As couples age, asynchronous sexuality becomes more common. For many couples, the sexual experience is better for the woman. Accepting this as normal and healthy is good for the woman, man, and couple. Even better, the man learns to piggy-back his arousal on hers.

The biggest challenge is to accept that 5–15% of sexual encounters are mediocre, dissatisfying, or dysfunctional. This is normal, not a sign of a sex problem. The self-defeating reaction is to panic or apologize which subverts sexual desire. Couples who believe in the intimacy/eroticism split or insist that every sexual experience be special and mutual eventually develop low desire. You become stuck in a blame–counter blame trap when your perfectionistic expectations are not met.

Responsive Sexual Desire for Women and Men

People think of desire in a simplistic manner—you are "hot" or you're not. This approach is magical and dominates your sexual life. In movies and novels desire is dramatic and intense, knowing no constraints or reality parameters. For men, the message is an erect penis has no conscience. It is as if desire is a primal urge which cannot be controlled.

In contrast, responsive sexual desire is not about drama. It is about openness and willingness. Responsive desire is about choice—are you receptive and responsive to touch with awareness of your feelings and your partner's feelings? On a 10-point scale of subjective pleasure, responsive desire is in the 2–4 range. When you are responsive to physical and emotional feelings, that is when you experience desire. Desire comes from your response to touching and to your partner's feelings. Desire is in response to the interaction rather than driven by spontaneous feelings.

There are many potential sources of sexual desire. Not all desire is responsive. Welcome and enjoy various sources of desire. However, with aging the majority of sexual desire is responsive.

A core strategy is awareness of bridges to desire. The concept of bridges to desire facilitates a mindful, planful approach to creating and nurturing desire. Examples of bridges to desire include receiving a sensual body massage, showering and enjoying playful touch, having a glass of wine sitting in front of the fireplace, reading poetry or a sexually explicit scenario, looking at old pictures, taking a nap and waking to your partner's sensual touch, having two beers as you listen to jazz, being sexual after a swim, watching an R- or X-rated video, sharing your favorite playful scenario. The function of bridges to desire is to facilitate awareness and receptivity.

Couples are open to both responsive and spontaneous desire. Desire can be open and exploratory or predictable and secure. As in much of sexuality it is not "right–wrong", but what is the right balance for you as a couple. The keys to desire are anticipation, sense of deserving, freedom and choice, and a mix of sexual scenarios and techniques. Desire at 70 is different than desire at 20 (which is about breaking boundaries and proving yourself sexually). Desire at 70 is about affirming yourself as a sexual person and feeling engaged as a couple. Sensual and playful touch promote responsive sexual desire.

Nola and Christopher

Christopher and Nola affirmatively answer the question of whether you can maintain desire in a long-term, secure marriage. They had been together for over 62 years, 59 as a married couple. They look forward to their 60th wedding anniversary. They are a religious couple who are a good marital and sexual model for their children and grandchildren. They are committed to a satisfying, secure, and sexual marriage for themselves, but not judgmental of others. They were supportive of their daughter who went through a difficult divorce. Nola and Christopher helped with grandchildren as their daughter reorganized her life. They felt empathy for their daughter and did not blame her or themselves for the divorce.

Nola and Christopher were surprised by the changing roles of sexuality during their relationship. They have very good memories of the pre-marital limerence phase when they had sex three times a day. Christopher thought it was a great experience even though the quality of the lovemaking was not good. Nola felt the magic of romantic love and passion made it special, although she agreed that the quality was mediocre. Both were surprised by the challenges of the first two years of marriage. Sex was a resource to help with the stresses of balancing careers and finances. Sex was often motivated by tension reduction.

Nola and Christopher found the four months of sex with the intention of getting pregnant to be an aphrodisiac. Christopher joked it was so much fun having sex every other day during the high probability week that he wished they'd had another two months before becoming pregnant. In terms of desire issues, the third trimester was challenging. She found intercourse in the man-on-top position awkward and uncomfortable. They tried woman on top, but Nola felt self-conscious about her stomach. Nola offered to pleasure Christopher to orgasm, but he wanted "real sex". During their second pregnancy two years later, they learned to value asynchronous sex. Christopher and Nola enjoyed being orgasmic with manual stimulation. They attended prepared childbirth classes. One of the couples suggested using sitting-kneeling intercourse because there was no pressure on the uterus and hands were free for multiple stimulation. Nola and Christopher used the sitting-kneeling intercourse position before and after the baby was born. It became one of their special scenarios. After several years Christopher developed knee problems so they stopped that intercourse position.

Christopher and Nola were a sexual couple throughout their parenting years. Many couples complain children interrupt sex and control their parents' sexual life. Nola and Christopher were committed to "beating the odds" and maintaining a vital, satisfying sexual relationship while parenting. A big surprise was that adolescent children had a more negative impact on sexual opportunities than did babies or toddlers. Privacy and maintaining personal boundaries allowed them to be sexual with teenagers in the house. Like most people, the "couple again" phase was an opportunity to revitalize sexual desire and satisfaction. Nola and

Christopher especially valued freedom to be sexual in different rooms in the house and at different times (rather than in the bedroom late at night). They particularly enjoyed sex during weekend getaways. Variable, flexible sexuality was facilitated by freedom of where, when, and how to be sexual. They have fond memories of this couple phase.

You cannot spend your life with someone without having to deal with sad or tragic events. One of the hardest experiences in life is the death of a child. Nola and Christopher had three children. Their middle child developed cancer when he was nine and died two years later. The three years after his death were the hardest of their lives. The challenge was to honor his memory while recommitting to their life, marriage, and family. Touching and sexuality were part of the grieving/healing process. During the cancer, sex was a tension reducer. For months after the death Christopher and Nola did a lot of crying and holding but had few sexual encounters. Intimacy, pleasuring, and eroticism were part of the healing process. A revitalized sexuality allowed them to feel present and engaged in life. The only time they were not sexual was on the son's birthday.

In her 50s Nola was diagnosed with type I breast cancer. Cancer is a disease of timing; early diagnosis and comprehensive treatment (surgery, radiation, and anti-estrogen medication) ensures a good prognosis. Christopher was there for Nola practically and emotionally. She asked him to accompany her to meetings with the oncologist, but after the initial meeting the physician declined to see them as a couple. A challenge was to avoid touching her infected breast. Nola experienced breast stimulation as anti-erotic. Nola accepted the new normal which included being sexual in the late afternoon/early evening because fatigue interfered with her sexual desire and response. Feeling desire and desirable was important for Nola.

With aging, Christopher was taking three medications. A major factor in low desire is side-effects of medications. Christopher's internist invited Nola for a couple consultation where they discussed Christopher's health, illnesses, and medications. This consultation and follow-up helped Christopher accept responsive desire as the right fit for him at this time. Nola was enthusiastic that her sexual response promoted his desire. It is never too late to adopt the Good Enough Sex (GES) approach. Rather than feeling demoralized by medical problems, Christopher and Nola approached this as a challenge to create a new couple sexual style.

Nola and Christopher dealt with psychological, biomedical, and relational challenges as an intimate sexual team. They hoped there would not be illness or crisis, but if it occurred, they would deal with it. Intimacy, pleasuring, and eroticism maintain sexual desire, especially with aging. Sexuality was a refuge—like a recharging station. They accepted each other as desirable sexual people, not based on visual attractiveness or dramatic eroticism, but on touch and sharing sensuality, playfulness, eroticism, and intercourse. Christopher valued intercourse as a symbol of being a sexual couple. In addition, erotic sexuality was satisfying for both. Nola enjoyed intercourse more for Christopher than for herself. She enjoyed a variety of sexual scenarios and techniques. Her erotic preference was receiving manual stimulation and self-entrancement arousal. They were committed to desire/pleasure/eroticism/satisfaction throughout their lives.

Maintaining Desire When Intercourse and Orgasm are Lessened

Is it possible to maintain sexual desire when you are no longer able to have intercourse? Absolutely yes. Is it possible to maintain sexual desire when you no longer experience orgasm? Absolutely yes. Is it possible to maintain sexual desire when you are no longer able to give and receive pleasure-oriented touch? This is a challenge, but is possible.

Let's start with intercourse. Enjoy intercourse, but intercourse does not define sex. Sensual, playful, and erotic scenarios enhance desire.

When one or both partners lose your erotic voice and are no longer orgasmic (including with self-stimulation during partner sex) this presents a challenge. It is a definite loss. We advocate for eroticism and orgasm, but the loss of orgasm does not kill desire. Touching continues to be a solid base for sexual desire.

Losing your sense of pleasure causes the end of desire for many, if not most, people, but it doesn't have to be so. You can anticipate a sexual encounter which is asynchronous—better for your partner. Enjoy your partner's pleasure and sexual response. This is emotionally and relationally rewarding even though you don't experience physical pleasure. Remember the psychobiosocial model of sexuality. Your major sex organ is your mind. Ideally, your mind and body are congruent in experiencing desire. Not feeling sexual pleasure is a true loss, but it doesn't make you a non-sexual person. You can feel desire psychologically and relationally. This is especially relevant to individuals with a chronic medical illness or disability. You still own your sexual desire.

Exercise: Maintaining Sexual Desire

Start this exercise with each partner establishing your "sexual voice". Next, focus on couple desire. This exercise has two phases: (1) Creating and reinforcing desire and (2) Maintaining resilient sexual desire.

For both men and women, low desire is usually a secondary dysfunction. Primary desire problems mean you have never anticipated or enjoyed couple sexuality. This is very rare for men, although it occurs when there is a sexual secret or a variant arousal pattern. You do not value intimate, interactive couple sexuality. For the great majority of men, desire problems are secondary. The major cause is sex dysfunction, especially erectile dysfunction. Female low desire is usually a secondary problem. However, there are a significant number of women who have sex at their partner's initiative but do not experience desire or pleasure for yourself. The more common problem is you have a history of desire (especially early in the relationship), but have lost your sexual voice.

In this exercise, the challenge is to identify and enhance sexual desire. Identify the psychological, biomedical, and social/relational factors which facilitate desire for you. Common psychological factors include self-esteem, feeling good about your life, awareness of bridges to desire, accepting yourself as a sexual person, valuing non-demand pleasuring, reading your favorite erotic stories, sex to compensate for a life disappointment, being proud of your aging process, enjoying masturbation and erotic fantasies, feeling pride in beating the odds, and sex as a symbol of thriving with a disability. Common biomedical factors which promote desire are feeling good about your aging body, being sexual before or after a nap, having a drink before sex, scheduling a couple consultation with your internist to alter medications and dosage so there is less impact on sexual response, maintaining healthy sleep, exercise, and eating patterns. Anything which is good for your physical body is good for your sexual body.

In terms of relational/social factors the strategy to facilitate desire is that both partners value intimacy and eroticism. This reinforces being intimate and erotic friends who share pleasure and eroticism. Attitudinally, valuing aging sexuality and commitment to "beating the odds" is empowering. Turning toward each other and accepting both synchronous and asynchronous scenarios reinforce sexual vitality. Being open to a range of sexual scenarios and techniques is important. Accept mediocre, dissatisfying, or dysfunctional sex rather than apologizing, blaming, or panicking. You are intimate and erotic friends in good and bad times. Be proud of being a sexual couple in your 60s, 70s, and 80s.

The second part of the exercise is crucial. What can you do to maintain sexual desire? Ultimately, desire is an interpersonal process. Sexual desire is surprisingly easy to kill in the couple context.

Focus on enhancing desire and addressing the problems which subvert desire. Responsive desire, especially with aging, is key. Specifically, being open to sensual and playful touch. Your partner's sexual receptivity and responsivity promotes your desire. The more bridges to desire (hers, his, and ours) the easier it is to maintain desire. Does that work in your relationship? What enhances desire for you—a date night, sex after watching an R-rated video, sex before or after a nap, sex for dessert after a meal and glass of wine? Does sex to reconnect after an argument, sex to spice up a boring day, sex to celebrate a birthday or anniversary, sex as a reward for completing your taxes, or sex as a reinforcer after a stressful encounter with your least favorite in-law serve to maintain desire? For you, what allows desire to thrive?

For many couples, a favorite bridge to desire is physical activity—a walk, bike ride, swim, golf. Then shower to make your body and genitals fresh for sex. What about sex as a refuge in dealing with sad or stressful life events? For example, after attending a funeral, sex in remembrance or as an affirmation of life. Can you look forward to sex after a consultation with your oncologist or after physical therapy (the desire to have a positive body experience)? What roles and meanings for touching and sexuality are inviting for you as a couple?

Be aware of what subverts desire and what you can do to counter that. The biggest barrier is clinging to the traditional approach of sex as an individual pass–fail performance test of erection and intercourse for the man and orgasm during intercourse for the woman. Adopt GES and embrace variable, flexible couple sexuality. A common negative factor is the traditional gender split with intimacy and eroticism. This results in a power struggle over who is at fault for low desire. The recommended strategy is integrative—both partners value intimacy and eroticism. Develop a healthy balance, congruent with your feelings and preferences. Another negative factor is the demand that all sex be mutual and equal. Accept asynchronous sex as well as synchronous sex. The demand that all sex be intimate, mutual, and functional burdens sexual desire.

The focus of this exercise is to promote strong, resilient sexual desire. We have recommended a variety of strategies and techniques. Find what is comfortable and inviting for you. Promote and maintain desire as an aging couple.

Summary

In the mantra of desire/pleasure/eroticism/satisfaction, desire is the core dimension. Desire is more important than sex frequency. The core of desire with aging is acceptance of broad-based, flexible, variable, pleasure-oriented touching. For both women and men, responsive sexual desire is healthier than hoping for spontaneous desire. To maintain desire, use all your psychological, biomedical, and social/relational resources to build anticipation with a focus on pleasure. GES expectations promote desire, especially acceptance of the multiple roles, meanings, and outcomes of sexuality. A key for men is accepting sensual, playful, and erotic scenarios as sexual rather than clinging to intercourse performance. A key for women is to embrace your sexual voice, including your erotic voice. Female sexuality is first class, not inferior to male sexuality. With aging, your sexual response is often easier and more predictable than his. You need each other sexually in a manner you did not 20 years before. Sexuality generally, and desire specifically, becomes more human and genuine with aging. Sexual desire is a couple process focused on touching and pleasure.

7

SATISFACTION: MORE THAN ORGASM

Orgasm is a natural continuation of the pleasure/eroticism process not a pass–fail performance test. Especially with aging, feeling good about the sexual experience is the best measure of satisfaction. The new understanding is crucial for males who have spent their whole life with the pattern of one orgasm during intercourse.

We are strong advocates for orgasm. However, orgasm is not the best measure of sexual satisfaction. Satisfaction centers on feeling good as a sexual person and energized as a sexual couple. The best sexual experience involves both partners, feeling high levels of desire/pleasure/eroticism/satisfaction. However, if that becomes a performance demand it ultimately subverts satisfaction. A crucial understanding is that sometimes the non-orgasmic partner can feel greater satisfaction than the orgasmic partner. Subjective satisfaction is a better measure than objective response (orgasm). Feeling good psychologically, relationally, and sexually is the best measure of satisfaction.

In the mantra of desire/pleasure/eroticism/satisfaction, satisfaction is the second most important dimension (desire is the most important). Satisfaction provides a framework to promote meaning for couple sexuality and illustrates the sexual paradox. Couple sexuality has a small, integral role for you and your relationship. It is a 15–20% factor to energize your bond. In contrast, sex dysfunction, conflict, and avoidance have an inordinately powerful negative role, demoralizing the individuals and threatening relational stability. When couples break up early in a marriage, sexual problems are the chief cause. Good sex cannot save a bad marriage, but bad sex can destroy a good marriage. Conflictual and dysfunctional sex is more powerful than good sex. The paradox is that dissatisfaction is much more impactful than satisfaction.

For some couples, marital stability is the controlling factor. Older couples usually do not divorce because of sex problems, but sexual dissatisfaction impacts your individual and relational well-being. The marriage remains stable but is not healthy. You miss the energizing role of touching and sexuality. Couples settle for stable marriages which feel "hollow". We advocate for satisfying, secure, and sexual marriage whether in your 30s or 70s.

Satisfying is the most important dimension. This illustrates the paradox—when sex is avoided it has an inordinately powerful role, robbing your relationship of energy and attachment. Sexuality promotes genuine attachment and special feelings. The key factor in satisfaction is feeling loved and accepted for who you are emotionally and sexually. It is not about sex performance and frequency (although we celebrate sexual function and a regular rhythm of sexual touching). Satisfaction is about feeling good about yourself as a person and bonded as a couple. Genuine attachment is core for satisfaction.

A measure of satisfaction is valuing affectionate, sensual, playful, and erotic touch in addition to intercourse. The operative concept is genuineness. A traditional female complaint is that sex is approached in a contingent or manipulative manner. Unless you meet his performance or frequency demands you won't be loved. Instead, you feel put down or made fun of. This power struggle negates satisfaction. The man feeling he needs to prove himself sexually negates genuine satisfaction. Rather than feeling accepted you have a contingent self-esteem and a contingent relationship. The foundation of satisfaction is acceptance of who you are as an aging person and couple. Acceptance is based on positive sexual attitudes and behaviors while accepting sexual vulnerabilities. Acceptance and satisfaction are based on reality, not on a "feel good" relationship or on "perfect" sexual response.

Good Enough Sex (GES) serves as the foundation for sexual expectations and acceptance. Ideally, sex is mutual and synchronous—both partners experience desire/pleasure/eroticism/satisfaction. However, that can't be a demand or expectation for all sexual encounters. Most sexual experiences are positive but asynchronous—better for one partner than the other. GES posits that 85% of encounters will flow to intercourse. When that does not occur, you transition to a sensual or erotic scenario. A crucial concept is understanding that not all sex needs to be synchronous or involve intercourse. Valuing asynchronous sexuality promotes satisfaction. When you experience a dissatisfying or dysfunctional sexual encounter, accept this rather than resorting to panic or blame. Satisfaction includes your ability to remain an intimate team when sex is disappointing or dysfunctional.

Satisfaction involves both objective and subjective factors. All couples can celebrate good sex. Healthy couples accept great sex, good sex, okay sex, mediocre sex, and dysfunctional sex.

Individual, Relational, and Sexual Dimensions of Satisfaction

It is crucial to understand individual, relational, and sexual dimensions of satisfaction. This confronts the simplistic criterion of intercourse and orgasm, replacing it with a nuanced and multi-dimensional understanding of couple sexuality. This is challenging, but crucial. A breakthrough experience is when one partner (typically the woman) is non-orgasmic yet feels more satisfied than the orgasmic partner. Subjective responsivity is more meaningful than objective response (orgasm).

A common trap for men is to use orgasm as a tension reducer rather than orgasm as an integral dimension of the pleasuring/eroticism process. The common trap for women is to work to achieve orgasm (especially during intercourse) and to view orgasm as an individual pass–fail performance. Orgasm for both genders is meaningful and satisfying when you experience both subjective and objective responsivity.

Barry remembers a couple who were highly conflictual about a range of issues, especially sexuality. The husband "worked to make her orgasmic during intercourse". At the therapy session, he enthusiastically reported she had "achieved orgasm" during intercourse. He believed this major breakthrough would revitalize their marriage. She looked at him with anger in her eyes and said, "My body betrayed me". Physically she was orgasmic, but it was against her will. She felt coerced and negated. The fact that he didn't understand her emotional reaction to orgasm made her feel even more negated. Although an extreme example, it illustrates the importance of subjective feelings regarding orgasm.

You own your sexual voice, including your orgasmic voice. When orgasm is a performance goal to prove something to self or partner this interferes with satisfaction. In the same way you share pleasure-oriented touching, share orgasm and satisfaction. This is true whether both partners are orgasmic, one partner is orgasmic, or neither partner is orgasmic.

A common issue is that orgasm is easier and more predictable for men (especially in young adulthood). This reinforces the myth that male sexuality is natural and superior. This mistaken belief develops in adolescence and young adulthood and reinforces the male–female double standard. This should have been challenged in your 20s and 30s, but it's never too late. Orgasm is not a competition with a winner and loser. Honor your orgasmic pattern as well as your partner's orgasmic pattern. Barry remembers a physician client who had a simplistic, destructive explanation for orgasm problems with his wife. He said, "I come too fast" and "She comes too slow". Identify and celebrate your orgasmic pattern, keeping in mind that orgasm is not the best measure of satisfaction. The most common male sex dysfunction is premature ejaculation (PE). He mistakenly attempts to reduce arousal with the hope that she will be orgasmic during intercourse. In fact, one in three women are never, or almost never, orgasmic during intercourse (Graham, 2014). He sets a performance goal to last ten minutes (or longer) so she can reach orgasm with intercourse. He tries to reduce his arousal by using two condoms, thinking anti-erotic thoughts (how much money he owes or about his mother-in-law), using a penile de-sensitizing cream, or barely thrusting. These arousal-reduction strategies are likely to cause desire problems for one or both partners. The average length of intercourse is three to nine minutes. For women who orgasm during intercourse the key is multiple stimulation (especially clitoral stimulation) before and during intercourse

(Mintz & Guitelman, 2020). Feeling badly because of PE reduces satisfaction. Learning ejaculatory control is a gradual couple process of increasing stimulation, not decreasing arousal. You learn to identify the point of "ejaculatory inevitability", after which orgasm is no longer under voluntary control. Learning ejaculatory control is a couple process oriented to sharing pleasure, not a performance test.

An advantage of aging is that for most men ejaculatory control improves without needing to engage in psychosexual skill exercises. With experience and feedback, you enjoy good (not perfect) ejaculatory control.

Female orgasmic response is variable, flexible, and individualistic. It is not a matter of better or worse but accepting your orgasmic pattern. From the base of acceptance you decide whether to add to your orgasmic pattern. The average woman is orgasmic during 70% of couple sexual encounters. The joke is that if sex were just about orgasm, both women and men would masturbate—a more reliable way to reach orgasm. By its nature, couple sexuality is variable and flexible. Accepting your orgasmic pattern involves expanding the roles and meanings of couple sexuality. Subjective satisfaction is more important than the physical sensations of orgasm.

This understanding of sexual response and satisfaction is more easily accepted by women than men. Similarities in desire/pleasure/eroticism/satisfaction are clearer with aging, as is awareness of the multiple roles, meanings, and outcomes of couple sexuality.

Delia and Terrence

This is a second marriage for both 81-year-old Delia and 82-year-old Terrence. Medically this is a challenging time in their lives, so satisfaction is a very meaningful topic. They had been married 22 years. Delia had been a widow for four years before meeting Terrence. She had not expected to remarry but was impressed with how empathic and kind Terrence was. He had been a caregiver to his wife as she dealt with cancer for six years before her death. Terrence began the mourning/grieving process as it became clear she would not survive this cancer.

He felt open to a second marriage. He was not looking for someone to replace his wife or to take care of him. His optimism and personal openness were an aphrodisiac for Delia. She had loved her deceased husband, but family was more fulfilling for her than the marriage. The husband had been a high performance, high sex frequency man who did not appreciate female sexuality. Sex was his domain and he felt sexually superior to Delia. She was more likely to be orgasmic during masturbation than intercourse (although she never discussed this with him). He complained to friends that even when he "went down on her" she didn't orgasm.

When Terrence and Delia began as a sexual couple, there was a great deal of awkwardness. Terrence wanted to be sure he didn't physically hurt Delia. This made her feel self-conscious and inhibited. Delia was used to the man controlling sex with the focus on intercourse. Feeling tentative and self-conscious is anti-erotic. Delia finally took the emotional risk and engaged in self-stimulation in front of Terrence. This was a new experience for both. He appreciated her willingness to share her way of experiencing pleasure, eroticism, and orgasm. Unlike the first husband, Terrence was open to her sexual feelings and preferences. Terrence was not just empathic, he was affirmative and valued couple sexuality. An involved, aroused partner is the major aphrodisiac. Sexual responsivity overcame shyness and tentativeness. Delia found her sexual voice as a 62-year-old woman. Terrence found her sexual receptivity and responsivity powerful. He did not compare sex in his second marriage with sex in the first marriage. Terrence and Delia developed a Complementary couple sexual style which combined with their Best Friend relational style. With aging, Terrence's orgasmic response was less stereotypic. He found it easiest and most satisfying to be orgasmic during intercourse from the man-on-top position, but was open to other positions and to Delia controlling thrusting. They engaged in multiple stimulation before and during intercourse. Both enjoyed orgasm with manual stimulation. As he aged, Terrence had more experiences when he was not orgasmic. If he stayed at it and worked hard, he would ejaculate, but it didn't feel satisfying. Instead, ejaculation was a relief to have sex over. Delia asked whether he was having fun sexually. Terrence was embarrassed, but said no—he was doing this so she wouldn't feel badly for him. Delia loved Terrence, especially his kindness, acceptance of her, and being pro-sexual. He didn't need an orgasm to prove anything to her. This was a great relief and allowed Terrence and Delia freedom to experiment with pleasuring, eroticism, and orgasm.

At age 81 Delia was medically healthy. Terrence exercised regularly, but it was a mile walk rather than a ten-mile bike ride. Each day, Terrence took a 40-minute nap. He was taking four medications on a regular basis. Delia was aware that within two to three years she would likely be a widow again.

Terrence was committed to maintaining couple sexuality as long as he lived. Delia was committed to being his intimate and erotic spouse. Being sexual with aging and illness is a rebellious act—sexuality affirms vitality. Terrence wanted Delia to join him in a broad-based approach to intimacy, pleasuring, and eroticism. Both had experienced the dying process of a spouse. Rather than feeling fearful it reinforced the value of touching and motivated them to enjoy relational vitality and satisfaction. Sex does not conquer death, but couple sexuality reinforces quality of life. At this point, Delia found orgasm easier and more satisfying than Terrence. He enjoyed asynchronous sexuality more than at any time in his life. Delia's sexual response enhanced his sexual satisfaction. He hoped to enjoy intimacy, pleasure, and eroticism until his death. Terrence was a kind and supportive partner. Delia joined him in affirming that satisfaction was much more than orgasm.

Kindness and vitality are quite different, but both contribute to the quality of life after 80. Delia was glad she'd overcome her fears and married Terrence. Their 22 years as a couple were emotionally and sexually satisfying.

The Paradox of Sexual Satisfaction

The role of couple sexuality with aging is paradoxical. Sexuality has a small, integral 15–20% role in energizing you and your bond. The paradox is that dysfunctional, conflictual, or avoidant sexuality has a powerful negative role. It isn't just missing sex; it robs you of a sense of attachment and intimacy. Avoidance gives sex a power it doesn't deserve. You lack a core connection—it is like driving a six-cylinder car, but only using four cylinders. Something vital is missing in your relationship. Lack of touch robs you of energy and satisfaction. When you stop intercourse you typically give up sensual, playful, erotic, and even affectionate touch. It is a major loss for the woman, man, and couple.

Professional colleagues tell us we are making too big a deal about sex, that it is not a core issue with aging. Health, finances, children, grandchildren, independent living vs. assisted living are much more important issues. We agree about the importance of attending to these issues, but we disagree that sexuality is less important. The majority of couples stop being sexual between 60 and 75. This is an unnecessary and poor choice. Stopping sex is not discussed, avoidance is not motivated by positive factors. The choice is made unilaterally because the man is frustrated and embarrassed. You avoid because you can't function sexually like you used to. Sex, especially predictable erections and intercourse, is not the way it was 20 years ago.

Turn to your partner for emotional and sexual support. A major issue is accepting loss of sexual predictability and control. Is satisfaction based on sex function and orgasm? If so, you are vulnerable. The challenge is to embrace GES. Sexual satisfaction is not based on control and orgasm. Our approach to satisfaction is in line with the lived experiences of women. Men cling to the old approach of control and orgasmic predictability. With aging, satisfaction is the crucial dimension in keeping both partners desirous and engaged. Couples who remain sexual in their 80s recognize touch, pleasure, eroticism, erotic flow, and orgasm as integral to your relationship. Although we advocate for pleasure and eroticism, the core dimensions are desire and satisfaction. Performance is an individual concept, pleasure and satisfaction are a couple concept. Turn toward your partner with a focus on satisfaction (which is more important than orgasm). This is true for both men and women.

Exercise: Strategies and Techniques to Enhance Satisfaction

Satisfaction is not "magic". You mindfully enhance individual and couple satisfaction. A key is focusing on what you value about sexuality. Satisfaction is not about how a sexual encounter ends, but how the experience plays out. Be specific about your sexual expectations—give honest answers not socially desirable ones. Identify emotional and physical factors that promote sexuality for you, do not split by traditional gender roles. Couples usually start with emotional factors such as closeness, love, and intimacy. Unless this is integrated with pleasuring and eroticism it will not promote satisfaction. The foundation of satisfaction is an integration of emotional and physical factors. It isn't a "right–wrong" struggle but valuing touching and integrating sexuality. Afterplay, especially sensual touch, promotes satisfaction. The sexual experience is balanced with emotional factors of openness, feeling desirable, and especially receptivity and willingness to engage. This integration is vital. Continuing physical stimulation to orgasm is not enough. Men 60 and older want a "happy ending", but working to achieve orgasm is seldom satisfying. In this exercise we encourage an honest dialogue which celebrates orgasm but focuses on emotional and sexual dimensions which enhance satisfaction.

What components of the encounter promote sexual satisfaction? The most common strategy is feeling "present", with awareness that the major aphrodisiac is an involved, responsive partner. This is an example of the value of partner interaction arousal. Being present also promotes self-entrancement arousal. Does this apply to you? Be clear what facilitates your satisfaction.

The third component is the orgasmic experience itself. There is a clear difference between a sexual experience where pleasure and eroticism flow to orgasm as opposed to a goal-oriented orgasm performance where orgasm is a relief rather than a pleasure. Don't try for a world-breaking orgasm, enjoy a satisfying sexual experience. Satisfying sexuality is more than the three to ten seconds of orgasm.

The final component of this exercise focuses on a commonly ignored issue—afterplay. Afterplay scenarios and techniques promote couple satisfaction. "Socially desirable" afterplay is alienating rather than satisfying. Short, ritual afterplay is neither genuine nor meaningful. What afterplay scenarios are meaningful for you? Do you enjoy afterplay which is playful, intimate, symbolic, nonverbal, sharing feelings, stroking your partner? Creative afterplay scenarios enhance satisfaction. You just experienced a physically intense encounter—now is the time to share emotional and physical bonding. Try one (or two) new afterplay scenarios to see whether it enhances your satisfaction. As with other components of couple sexuality, if it does not have the hoped-for results, that is important to recognize. It motivates you to try a different scenario to promote satisfaction. This is not a competition or a performance. What enhances your satisfaction?

Dealing with Dissatisfying or Dysfunctional Encounters

It is one thing to abstractly say that it is normal for 5–15% of sexual experiences to be disappointing or dysfunctional. Your challenge is to implement this new understanding. The common reaction is to apologize or blame. This gives the experience more power than it deserves and further reduces satisfaction. Turn toward your partner and accept that the encounter was problematic. Ideally, you laugh or at least shrug it off. It is normal to have "bad sex". Negative sexual experiences do not define you personally or as a couple. Accept dissatisfying or dysfunctional sex while being a resilient sexual team. This is critical for sexual desire and satisfaction.

When I first became involved in the sex therapy field, I was in my late 20s. My approach focused on restoring sex function. In retrospect, I had the sequencing wrong. Begin with sexual acceptance. From there you build sexual comfort and confidence focused on pleasure. Commitment to a couple process of sharing pleasure leads to increased sexual confidence and function. Break the cycle of contingent sexual self-esteem. Personal and couple sexuality is based on sharing pleasure, not perfect performance. This is more than a change in wording, it signifies changes in sexual attitudes, behavior, feelings, and values. Sexual satisfaction is based on an acceptance model rather than a performance model. Loss of intercourse or orgasm does not mean you lose sexual satisfaction. Subjective satisfaction is more important than objective sex function, especially with aging.

Pride in Beating the Odds and Affirming Couple Sexuality

When I present workshops for couple therapists and mental health professionals the concept of desire/pleasure/eroticism/satisfaction is well received. However, invariably an older male clinician will approach me and say, "Good presentation but we both know that you need intercourse and orgasm". I am not adversarial, but say, "Scientifically, clinically, and personally I believe what I say—you can enjoy couple sexuality which does not involve intercourse or orgasm". This is core to implementing GES. The clinician steps back and usually agrees professionally, but you can tell that it doesn't penetrate personally. As long as he has predictable sex function he is not open to accepting satisfaction based on GES. Even if he knows that this is scientifically true, he feels less manly accepting that satisfaction is not dependent on sex performance. This is true even for clinicians who accept the concept of responsive male sex desire. Satisfaction that is not based on performance feels like a "bridge too far". We believe a "both–and" approach is key for satisfaction. You celebrate intercourse and orgasm as well as accept non-orgasmic, non-intercourse sexuality. Couple sexuality is not a zero-sum game. A key to satisfaction is embracing a range of sexual experiences, meanings, and outcomes.

Summary

In the mantra of desire/pleasure/eroticism/satisfaction, satisfaction is the second most important dimension. Satisfaction includes orgasm, but orgasm is not the core component. Orgasm can be a misleading measure. The essence of satisfaction is feeling good about yourself as a sexual person and energized as a sexual couple. Rather than orgasm as an individual measure of objective function, satisfaction is both a subjective and objective measure which integrates emotional and physical components. Satisfaction connotes genuineness and meaning. An excellent example is the situation where the non-orgasmic partner found the experience highly satisfying while the orgasmic partner did not feel satisfied. When one partner has to work to achieve orgasm, the experience is more a relief than a shared pleasure. Satisfaction is highest when intimacy, pleasure, and eroticism flow to orgasm.

Afterplay scenarios and techniques enhance personal and couple satisfaction. Afterplay is particularly valuable when it reflects genuine meaning, whether intimate, playful, or energizing (not a routine ritual). Afterplay is a validation of you as a sexual couple. Traditionally, afterplay was viewed as the woman's domain and not important for the man. With aging, afterplay, like so many other sexual factors, reflects sexuality as a shared domain. Afterplay is a bonding experience valued by both partners. Afterplay reinforces satisfaction as a key to sexuality with aging.

8

NAKED AT OUR AGE: THE CHALLENGE OF INTEGRATED EROTICISM

Traditional sexual socialization involved a split between eroticism (the man's domain) and intimacy (the woman's domain). This split reinforced the male–female double standard which is harmful for men, women, couples, and the culture. The intimacy/eroticism split is especially harmful for couple sexuality with aging. The mantra of desire/pleasure/eroticism/satisfaction challenges the intimacy/eroticism and female/male splits.

Culturally, erotic scenarios emphasize role enactment arousal illustrated in porn videos and "kink" scenarios. An empowering concept is integrated eroticism which focuses on partner interaction and self-entrancement arousal. Eroticism is integrated in your relationship. The man, woman, couple, and culture embrace eroticism as integral to sexuality. This is particularly relevant for sexuality and aging. The trap is to de-eroticize aging couples, especially women. The erotic theme is high-intensity sex driven by illicitness and visual stimuli. If portrayed at all, aging sexuality centers on emotional closeness and affection, not erotic feelings and scenarios.

Integrated eroticism is a foreign notion in our culture generally, much less applied to aging couples. Integrated eroticism motivates you to create a couple sexual style which is the right fit for you. In our culture, couples feel intimidated rather than empowered by the traditional approach to eroticism. The message is that you are not erotic enough, especially compared to what is portrayed in porn videos or employed by sex workers. Intimidation is especially evident with older couples who are de-eroticized in our culture. The message is that eroticism belongs to young, new, and illicit couples. This self-defeating approach must be confronted. You are an erotic couple whether 65, 85, or 25. Eroticism is an integral, valued part of your sexual voice and shared in your relationship. Eroticism is a core component of the desire/pleasure/eroticism/satisfaction mantra.

Eroticism is associated with sexual vitality. It is integrated into couple sexuality, not an isolated dimension. Integrated eroticism applies to mainstream couples, not reserved for new, illicit, and dramatic relationships. This challenges the de-eroticization of older couples. The narrow definition of eroticism is based on the mistaken belief that eroticism is the domain of dramatic sexuality and knows no boundaries. It requires perfect sex, visual stimuli, and illicitness. This is a self-defeating approach to eroticism and aging.

The Core of Eroticism for Couples Over 60

The core of eroticism is intense feelings and physical sensations—subjective arousal levels 6–10. Eroticism values sharing sexual intensity. It is integrated, not isolated. Individually and as a couple own your eroticism. Eroticism is based primarily on touch stimuli, not visual stimuli. You can enjoy eroticism in your 60s, 70s, and 80s (although the dimensions are somewhat different). Aging sexuality is not just about intimacy and pleasuring. Fully functioning sexuality includes eroticism. Women and men celebrate eroticism integrated with intimacy and pleasuring. Pleasuring leads to eroticism, but sometimes eroticism is the lead dimension. We advocate for the pleasuring/eroticism process, but that is not the only way to experience eroticism. Free-standing eroticism has a role in couple sexuality. Do not apologize for embracing intense sensations and feelings.

The Three Styles of Arousal/Eroticism

The three arousal/eroticism styles are:

1. Partner interaction arousal/eroticism
2. Self-entrancement arousal/eroticism
3. Role enactment arousal/eroticism

These are very different, but not incompatible, ways of sharing arousal/eroticism (Mosher, 1980). Partner interaction arousal is the most commonly utilized—your arousal is enhanced by your partner's arousal. Like an erotic dance, each partner's arousal feeds the other's. This extends the "give to get" pleasuring process to the erotic process. The major aphrodisiac is an involved, aroused partner. This is the type of arousal portrayed in R-rated movies. Partner interaction arousal/eroticism reinforces giving and receiving erotic touch and active involvement in erotic scenarios.

Self-entrancement arousal/eroticism involves a scenario where one partner is giver and the other receiver. Use of self-entrancement arousal increases with aging. A core understanding is the receiving partner is not passive but mindful and actively focuses on erotic feelings and sensations. Self-entrancement arousal is very different than foreplay where the receiving partner is passive and it is the man's job to turn her on. In self-entrancement arousal the receiving partner actively welcomes eroticism. Although you usually switch roles, that is not a necessary component. Self-entrancement arousal increases with aging because it is a non-demanding way to elicit arousal. This illustrates the importance of being open and receptive as opposed to "doing the partner". The giving partner is not responsible for the receiving partner's sexual response but enjoys providing erotic touch and is open to your feedback. The receiving partner is mindful of taking in erotic sensations and feelings—going with erotic flow without self-consciousness or inhibitions.

Role enactment arousal/eroticism involves using external stimuli to enhance arousal. This is the eroticism style celebrated on the internet and in sex clubs. However, it is the least practiced, especially with older couples. Role enactment arousal promotes risk-taking and sexual vitality. The issue is not a "right–wrong" way to celebrate eroticism, but what is erotically inviting for you.

Most couples favor partner interaction arousal/eroticism not just because you are used to it, but you welcome integrated eroticism. It reinforces being erotic allies and promotes mutual arousal. Men learn to piggy-back your arousal on her arousal. Each partner's arousal facilitates the other's. This reinforces engagement and vitality.

Role enactment arousal uses external stimuli as an erotic charge. This "spices up" your sexual relationship by enhancing unpredictability. Usually, the erotic scenario is more charged for one partner than the other. Role enactment arousal/eroticism is asynchronous which is as it should be. Seldom do partners have the exact same erotic preferences. Examples of external stimuli include watching a porn video together, using sex toys like a paddle or vibrator, blindfolding your partner, tying up the spouse, a power play where you are totally passive, videotaping the sexual scenario, acting out an erotic fantasy. Emotionally Expressive sexual style couples are most open to role enactment arousal. Sex is inviting as long as each partner has the right to veto a scenario. Role enactment arousal emphasizes risk-taking, breaking boundaries, and feeling "naughty". For example, some people find "dirty" language a turn-on. As long as the erotic scenario is not harmful to the partner or relationship it promotes sexual vitality.

Most aging couples utilize partner interaction arousal/eroticism and a growing number use self-entrancement arousal/eroticism. Some couples experiment with role enactment arousal/eroticism on occasion as a "special treat".

Be aware of the value of integrated eroticism as a shared domain. The challenge is to determine the best blend of intimacy, pleasuring, and eroticism which is right for you. This is likely to change over time and circumstances. It is critical that eroticism remains in your relationship. Eroticism is integral to couple sexuality.

Andrea and Matt

Matt's first marriage lasted 41 years until his wife died after seven years of ill health. Matt was a loyal spouse. With his wife in failing health Matt accepted the non-sexual state of their marriage. Masturbation was his sexual outlet. Matt missed couple sexuality, but masturbation was erotic, not just a tension reducer.

Andrea had a very different sexual history. Her first marriage ended after 22 years with the death of her husband in a drunk driving accident.

Sex had been his domain, not physically or emotionally fulfilling for Andrea. The focus was on intercourse which the husband tried to extend, but he usually ejaculated in less than two minutes. This was fine with Andrea who did not find intercourse arousing. "Foreplay" was even less enjoyable. Andrea did not have a "sexual voice". As a widow Andrea found sex with other men unsatisfying. The partner often had erectile problems and she had to work to get him aroused. Sometimes, he would lose his erection. Andrea couldn't decide if the sex problem was his fault, her fault, or they did not fit as a couple.

Matt was 68 and Andrea 65 when they met. They were at a bridge tournament organized by mutual friends. Both enjoyed bridge with its competitiveness and camaraderie. Matt was open to a new relationship, but Andrea was not interested. Over time they became platonic friends who shared bridge, hiking, and volunteering for community causes. Andrea saw Matt as a nice man who was lonely and needed a relationship. He told her of his dating experiences which often were disastrous. She said he was "looking for love in all the wrong places". Matt became trapped in a manipulative relationship. Andrea confronted Matt about this unhealthy relationship and helped him navigate its end. At the termination, the woman said very harsh things to Matt. Andrea encouraged him to dismiss these destructive judgments.

On the next group hike a grateful Matt told Andrea how much he appreciated her help and he wanted to date her. Matt made it sound inviting, and Andrea was interested except for her fear this would lead to the same sexual dead-end. For the first time, Andrea discussed her history of disappointing sex. Matt listened respectfully and didn't try to talk her out of it or overpromise that he was a great lover. He valued affectionate and sensual touch and promised to not push her sexually. She could veto a touching experience and he would honor her veto. Andrea had not talked about intimacy and sexuality like this with any man. She was impressed that Matt did not just "talk the talk" he "walked the walk". Her confidence grew as did her welcoming of touch. They did not use the phrase "non-demand pleasuring", but that was what was happening. When Matt had an erection, she didn't feel pressured. His erection was a sign of pleasure not a demand for intercourse. Andrea did not like being passive when Matt touched her. She preferred partner interaction arousal. She was more responsive to his touch when she was actively touching him.

One day both were feeling sexually responsive. Matt did not want to break the touching rhythm or put pressure on Andrea. He asked if he could do self-stimulation to orgasm while she held him. Andrea was surprised and intrigued. No man had ever asked this of her but, instead, would push intercourse. Andrea knew if she said no Matt would accept that. Knowing she did not have to say yes Andrea was surprised that she found holding him while he engaged in self-stimulation arousing. Afterward she felt closer. She was open to his playful touch, including breast and thigh touching. Andrea took off her bra, leaving the rest of her clothes on. As they talked, Matt told her how much he enjoyed erotic touch. It was not just to reach orgasm; he genuinely valued the erotic experience. This is not something Andrea had ever felt. Her experience was that erotic touch was for the man and always led to intercourse. Matt wanted her to enjoy integrated erotic touch. They would progress at her comfort level.

They grew as an intimate couple. Andrea became comfortable pleasuring him to orgasm and enjoyed that asynchronous experience. She liked taking off his clothes and touching his naked body. It was not a visual turn-on but was a touch turn-on. She enjoyed his sexual response and increasingly felt open to his touch. Andrea preferred leaving her underpants on when receiving genital touch. She put her hand over Matt's and guided him on the types of touch she enjoyed. Although both wanted to add intercourse, they were hesitant because of fear it would disrupt their erotic rhythm. They worried that intercourse would dominate couple sexuality and be a disappointment.

A major breakthrough was Andrea's allowing pleasuring/erotic stimulation to flow to orgasm with Matt's manual stimulation. Andrea enjoyed sexual responsivity rather than feeling pressured.

This erotic experience was a great leap forward—she became freer and open to erotic flow. As her arousal built, she said "I want you inside me". This was a powerful invitation for Matt. For the first time Andrea was enjoying intercourse. Like one in three women, Andrea's arousal and orgasm pattern was with manual (and later oral) stimulation rather than intercourse. The change is she now enjoyed intercourse.

Eroticism is not about everything being equal or working perfectly. Andrea was receptive and responsive to Matt's manual and oral stimulation. Andrea was uncomfortable giving oral stimulation. She was afraid Matt would feel she was "sexually selfish". It is anti-erotic to believe everything needs to be equal. Matt honored Andrea's veto about giving oral stimulation. Andrea receiving manual and oral stimulation, partner interaction arousal, self-entrancement arousal, and intercourse were positive. Her favorite erotic scenario was being orgasmic with manual stimulation before intercourse. Matt validated that. They enjoyed integrated eroticism in their 70s and 80s. If intercourse was not functional for Matt, they transitioned to an erotic scenario which was satisfying for both. They adopted the Complementary couple sexual style which promoted desire/pleasure/eroticism/satisfaction. For the first time since his wife became ill, Matt felt he was in a healthy relationship where intimacy, pleasuring, and eroticism were integrated. Andrea felt for the first time in her life that she was in a vital, satisfying relationship where her erotic voice was heard and honored.

Erotic Challenges for Women

There are many more sexual similarities than differences between aging women and men. A major challenge is to own your erotic voice rather than apologize for your eroticism (McCarthy & McCarthy, 2018). Porn depictions emphasize "crazy" women swept away by intense sexual feelings (sexual drama with no boundaries and no negative consequences). This represents the traditional belief that eroticism is for men, but dangerous for women. Only "bad girls" are erotic. Another powerful cultural message is that rape, sexual abuse, and negative sexual consequences are the woman's fault. Last, aging women cannot be erotic, this is for young, foolish women. What a self-defeating approach to female eroticism.

In contrast, we are strong advocates for the aging woman to own your erotic voice. Embrace the challenge to be naked at your age (Price, 2011).

This is healthy for you and your relationship. You are a sexual woman from the day you are born to the day you die. Confront myths and fears. Embrace vital, erotic sexuality. Often, your approach to eroticism is different than your partner's. Do not assume that his approach is better. You are not erotic clones of each other. It is normal and healthy to have different erotic preferences. Create your preferred erotic scenarios—he will find it a turn-on because you feel turned-on. He can veto an erotic scenario which is a turn-off for him. Likewise, you can veto a scenario which is a turn-off for you. It is easier to accept female–male sexual equity when discussing desire, sensuality, pleasure, and satisfaction. It is more of a challenge discussing eroticism. Identify shared attitudes, behaviors, emotions, and values regarding eroticism. Your erotic voice is as important as his. Take advantage of the freedom to express your preferences for erotic scenarios and techniques.

Erotic Challenges for Men

A common theme is men feeling you aren't good enough sexually, especially erotic performance. For adolescent and young adult men the theme is not having enough erotic experiences with sexually crazy women. For middle-years men the theme is you've settled for marital sex and don't have enough erotic experiences. You are not sexually dominant as are the men in porn videos and don't have large and dependable erections. The theme for men over 60 is you are "over the hill" erotically.

What is the erotic reality? Eroticism is a shared domain. Being erotic friends and allies promotes couple sexuality. A particular challenge with aging is that male sexual response becomes more variable and less predictable, including erections, intercourse, and orgasm. Often, this increases performance anxiety, leading to sexual avoidance. You can adopt an approach to unpredictability which serves as a cue to enhance pleasure and eroticism. Learn to piggy-back your arousal on her arousal, an example of partner interaction arousal/eroticism. This is a powerful erotic strategy. Her arousal facilitates your arousal and her arousal is facilitated by realizing you need her sexual responsivity and vitality. This is a winning strategy for both partners. Wise men embrace integrated eroticism and enjoy this chapter of your sexual life.

Exercise: Integrating Eroticism with Your Aging Process

This exercise challenges you to develop erotic scenarios and techniques which enhance sexuality with aging. Each person states preferences for partner interaction arousal/eroticism, self-entrancement arousal/eroticism, and/or role enactment arousal/eroticism. Do you agree on your preferred style(s)? Is there a style you want to downplay or eliminate? The best time to dialogue about erotic preferences is in a therapist's office where you are clear and specific, not anxious or defensive. The second-best place is in your home the day before a sexual encounter. You are dressed and sitting over a cup of tea or glass of wine (one glass, not a bottle). The worst time to talk eroticism is lying nude in bed after a negative sexual encounter—it is too easy to blame and put-down. Discussing erotic scenarios and techniques is challenging but is of great value. In addition to preferences, it is crucial that each partner has the power to veto an erotic scenario or technique that is not acceptable. Unless you have the power to say no you do not have the freedom to say yes to erotic sexuality. Do not approach this exercise in a socially desirable or politically correct manner. Accept the challenge to develop and maintain genuine eroticism. What are you willing to explore to enhance eroticism in your life?

Are you more likely to feel erotic if you begin with pleasurable, playful, or erotic scenarios? The issue is what fits you, not worrying about the "right" way. Once you decide on the arousal/erotic style that is the best fit, focus on specific scenarios—manual sexuality, oral sexuality, intercourse sex, anal sexuality, rubbing sexuality. Do you prefer taking turns, mutual stimulation, or improvise and go with the flow? Do intimate, playful, and/or lustful feelings add to your experience? When it comes to erotic flow (feelings and sensations in the 8–9 range), do you prefer one partner in charge, a mutual experience, or being open to however it plays out?

A crucial question is whether verbal or non-verbal communication promotes your erotic experience. Be honest—what is true for you? Some couples utilize sounds, others romantic or explicit language, others let your body do the talking. Discussing this in a non-sexual context makes it easier to translate in an erotic context.

For you is eroticism about nudity, sexy clothing, informal outfits, fancy clothing? Does starting nude facilitate or inhibit eroticism? Do you like your partner to take off your clothes, do you like taking off their clothes, or would you rather take off your own clothes? Do environmental cues (candles, music, dim lights, mirrors) facilitate eroticism? Is privacy erotically inviting or do you experience an erotic charge if you might be discovered? Do not assume—share and ask your partner their feelings and preferences.

The second part of this exercise requires more of you—implement what you discussed. People fear that discussing and processing robs the scenario of its erotic charge. It is true that self-consciousness is anti-erotic. However, comfort, openness, and awareness enhance eroticism. Finding the right balance is key to implementing erotic scenarios and techniques. Enjoy pleasure, arousal, eroticism, erotic flow, and orgasm. Self-consciousness or demanding a sex performance undermines eroticism. On a 10-point scale of subjective arousal, eroticism begins at 6, erotic flow 8–9, with 10 orgasm. Let yourself go with the erotic flow. In partner interaction eroticism your arousal enhances your partner's arousal. In self-entrancement eroticism you enjoy erotic feelings and sensations which flow to orgasm.

Implement your chosen erotic scenarios and techniques. Enjoy the process. If something is not inviting switch to a different erotic scenario or end the experience with a sensual or playful scenario.

Do not expect every experience to be erotic. Perfection is for novels and movies, not real-life couple sexuality with aging. In implementing this exercise remember the GES guideline—85% of scenarios will include erotic feelings. In addition, enjoy experiences which are sensual and pleasurable even if not erotic.

Summary

Your challenge with aging is to value the desire/pleasure/eroticism/satisfaction mantra. Eroticism is the most contentious dimension because throughout adulthood eroticism was the man's domain, not a shared domain. The culture emphasizes dramatic eroticism portrayed in porn and role enactment arousal/eroticism. This intimidates older couples rather than welcomes erotic sexuality. Integrated eroticism is key. Affirm partner interaction arousal/eroticism and with increasing frequency self-entrancement arousal/eroticism. Sex is better when the woman has a clear erotic voice, the man has his erotic voice, and eroticism is valued in your relationship.

Erotic scenarios and techniques are valued, but not as a performance to prove something to yourself or your partner. Unless you have the power to say no to an erotic scenario, you do not have the freedom to enjoy integrated eroticism. Erotic scenarios are usually asynchronous. Asynchronous eroticism energizes your bond.

Usually pleasure, arousal, and eroticism flow, but this is not the only way to express eroticism.

Eroticism for aging couples emphasizes touch stimuli rather than visual stimuli. Some couples use role enactment arousal, including acting out sexual fantasies. Most eroticism is based on partner interaction or self-entrancement arousal. Don't compare your aging erotic experience with the romantic love/passionate sex/idealization (limerence) phase. Own your erotic experiences as an aging couple.

Eroticism energizes your bond. You cheat yourself and your relationship when you limit sex to intercourse. Whether the erotic experience involves intercourse or focuses on manual, oral, rubbing, or vibrator stimulation, eroticism affirms couple sexuality. Enjoy eroticism which flows to intercourse, as well as erotic experiences that do not involve intercourse. Eroticism includes orgasm, but not orgasm as a performance. Letting go and enjoying high-intensity feelings and sensations is the core of eroticism.

9

COUPLE SEXUALITY: VALUING SYNCHRONOUS AND ASYNCHRONOUS SEXUALITY

The best sex is mutual and synchronous. This means both partners experience high levels of desire/pleasure/eroticism/satisfaction. Mutual sexual expression is highly valued. However, most sexual experiences are asynchronous. This means the sexual encounter was positive, but better for one partner than the other. With aging, asynchronous sexual experiences become more common. A particular challenge is the gender reversal—sex is often easier and more satisfying for the woman than the man. With young couples, asynchronous sex was usually better for the man. Accepting this change is a challenge for both partners, especially the man. The good news is that you can learn to piggy-back your arousal on hers. This is a plus for both partners. Her sexual response enhances yours. Sexuality is more genuine and human with aging. You need each other in a way you did not 20 years before.

Couples affirm both synchronous and asynchronous experiences. You want to not just enjoy asynchronous sexuality but celebrate it. Asynchronous sexuality is healthy as long as it is not at the expense of the partner or your relationship. Synchronous and asynchronous sexual experiences are complementary, not competitive. If all sex had to be mutual and synchronous, there would be an increase in low-sex relationships. You are not sexual clones of each other. Sex can have different roles, meanings, and outcomes for each person rather than demanding that all sex be synchronous. Sexual variability and flexibility is of value, especially with aging.

An advantage of sexuality and aging is freedom to enjoy a range of experiences rather than being burdened by routine, predictable, performance-oriented sex. Different scenarios and variations in sexual pleasure and eroticism are welcomed. This makes sex more interesting. Intercourse is more likely to be synchronous, especially for couples who accept the woman's orgasmic preferences whether before, during, or after intercourse.

Women are more likely to accept asynchronous sexuality because it is congruent with your lived sexual experiences. Female sexual response is variable and flexible. Men learn sexual response as highly predictable—a single orgasm during intercourse. Female orgasmic response might involve a single orgasm, multiple orgasms, or being non-orgasmic. Orgasm may come from manual, oral, intercourse, vibrator, or rubbing stimulation. Orgasm is not the best measure of synchronous sex. Although the majority of women are orgasmic during intercourse, rarely are you orgasmic 100% of the time. The range is between 30–90% of couple encounters. The average is 70% (Graham, 2014). Be aware that there are sexual encounters where you are non-orgasmic but feel emotionally satisfied. There are times that although the man was orgasmic, he did not feel emotionally or sexually satisfied.

Approximately one in three women are never or almost never orgasmic during intercourse, but are reliably orgasmic with erotic stimulation. This is a normal and healthy pattern. A theme of aging sexuality is that sexual response is more variable and flexible for both partners. A second theme is that subjective arousal is more important than objective arousal (vaginal lubrication, erection, orgasm). This can be confusing but need not be. Rather than view sex as a simple pass–fail individual performance, sexuality with aging is best understood as a couple process of sharing pleasure with a range of roles, meanings, and outcomes. The Good Enough Sex (GES) model is motivating and helps you accept your sexual experiences (McCarthy & Metz, 2008). This includes accepting synchronous and asynchronous sexuality as well as occasional sexual dissatisfaction or dysfunction. That too is part of normal sexuality with aging. Aging is a powerful antidote to associating sex and performance. If you cling to a perfectionistic, performance approach you are setting yourself up to be a non-sexual couple.

The Joys of Synchronous Sex

Synchronous couple sexuality is a source of joy and satisfaction. The core of synchronous sex is sharing desire/pleasure/eroticism/satisfaction. This is true whether you have intercourse or not. Most aging couples continue to value intercourse (especially true for men). The ideal synchronous sexual experience involves responsive sexual desire, the give and take of pleasuring which flows to arousal, eroticism including orgasm, and feeling bonded and energized as an intimate couple. Synchronous sexuality involves freedom from sexual performance demands. In synchronous sex both partners embrace sexuality which celebrates desire/pleasure/eroticism/satisfaction.

The Joys of Asynchronous Sexuality

Affirming the positive role of asynchronous sexuality is crucial throughout life, especially with aging. Be aware that most sexual experiences are asynchronous. This means it is positive for both partners, but better for one than the other. In younger years, asynchronous sex was better for the man. After 60, asynchronous sexual experiences are often (not always) better for the woman. This gender transition is a challenge. Knowing your sexual responsivity is good for your partner is motivating. He piggybacking his arousal on yours is new and enhances couple sexuality. With aging, sexuality is more of an intimate team experience. The good things in couple sexuality come to fruition with aging. Asynchronous sex is an example of variable, flexible couple sexuality. Not all sexual experiences need to be mutual or equal.

Asynchronous sex demonstrates that you are not sexual clones. Sexual encounters have different motivations and outcomes. This understanding is affirming for the woman, man, and couple. For one partner the sexual encounter is about sharing intimacy, for the other it is a tension reducer. For one sex is to affirm couple vitality, for the other it is to share sensuality. These are examples of different sexual motivations and meanings. Acceptance and freedom are hallmarks of sexuality with aging.

Lydia and Juan

When they met 26 years ago, 55-year-old Lydia had been a widow for five years and 50-year-old Juan had been divorced from his second wife for almost seven years. They are an example of the challenges and strengths of couples from different ethnic, religious, and economic backgrounds. When challenges are recognized you are a stronger couple. Lydia came from a working-class Polish-American background and with her first husband established a family based on a traditional life organization. There was much Lydia assumed about working-class life and marriage, including the belief that sex was the man's prerogative and that the family was the woman's domain. Most sexual experiences were asynchronous, which Lydia believed was normal. She would occasionally be orgasmic during afterplay, but most of the time "went along for the ride". She was the primary parent and pleased that both her daughters graduated college and created middle-class families. After the funeral of their father, both daughters affirmed their love and respect for Lydia.

Lydia had no expectation that she would remarry but enjoyed working in the hotel industry. She dated occasionally and was surprised by her sexual responsivity during a sexual friendship. She recognized that like many of her friends she was most responsive to erotic stimulation. She preferred kissing, oral breast stimulation, manual clitoral stimulation and, when subjective arousal was 7 or greater, oral stimulation to orgasm.

Lydia would rather be single than in a poor-quality marriage. She recognized that mediocrity was the reality of many marriages, including her own. Neither the husband nor she thrived in that marriage.

Juan's life experiences were quite different. He moved to the United States as a child and was undocumented. His 19-year-old American girlfriend became pregnant, they married, and he obtained a green card. Three years later he became a U. S. citizen. A year after that they had a bitter divorce where she accused him of marrying so he could obtain citizenship. Juan was angry at having his motivations negated. In retrospect, he regretted that marriage, but not their son. Four years later he became the custodial parent and was immensely proud of his son's achievements, especially the son's career and family. Juan had a second marriage that lasted less than two years. After that, he gave up on marriage until he met Lydia. At her insistence they discussed psychological, relational, and sexual histories. Neither wanted an unhealthy relationship. Juan regretted his relational past but was not ashamed of it.

Like many middle-years couples, Lydia and Juan began as sexual friends without unrealistic hopes. Sex was not the most important factor in their relationship. They had a serious dialogue about intimacy and sexuality. Healthy sexuality and a healthy relationship are reciprocally reinforcing.

Juan's son and daughter-in-law were very fond of Lydia and urged Juan to be open to a serious relationship, whether marriage or a life partnership. Juan had done very well professionally. He was a general contractor with a specialty in restoring historic homes. He employed a multi-ethnic work crew; expertise was more important than ethnic background. Lydia admired that Juan hired and trained men who had been incarcerated.

They dialogued about differences in backgrounds, religion, relational history, finances, sexual values, and life organization. Juan loved his work and hoped to continue until at least 75. Lydia did not want to be thought of as a "gold digger" or feel financially dependent. They were aware of their complicated emotional and sexual histories. They wanted a relationship where each felt valued for who they were in the present. Processing the past is healthy as long as you don't punish yourself or feel judged by your spouse. You cannot change the past but can learn from it. Lydia and Juan committed to creating a healthy relationship, including sexually. Lydia was clear that she didn't want to settle for sex that was unsatisfying. Juan agreed that the routine of foreplay to get Lydia ready for intercourse and prolonging intercourse so she could reach orgasm was not an inviting scenario for either of them. When they transitioned from being a dating couple to marriage, one challenge was developing a satisfying couple sexual style. This included building sexual anticipation, especially bridges to desire. Rather than Juan always being the initiator, both could initiate with a focus on giving and receiving pleasure-oriented touching. Goal-oriented foreplay with Lydia being passive was not acceptable. She was most likely to be orgasmic with a combination of manual and oral stimulation while she was touching Juan. He celebrated her orgasmic pattern rather than expecting her to have a single orgasm during intercourse as he did. Juan, like most men after 60, developed a variable orgasmic pattern. Juan and Lydia enjoyed mutual manual stimulation to orgasm. This became their favorite synchronous sexual scenario. Juan's favorite asynchronous scenario involved intercourse where he was orgasmic and Lydia was not, but she was involved and enjoyed touching. As they aged intercourse was less reliable but was highly valued. A common synchronous scenario was Lydia being orgasmic before intercourse with Juan orgasmic during intercourse. Lydia enjoyed intercourse more when she had an orgasm during the pleasuring phase.

Lydia enjoyed erotic scenarios where her sexual responsiveness was easier than his. This was a challenge, but with practice and feedback Juan learned to piggy-back his arousal on hers. Usually, he was aroused enough for intercourse, but when not, they transitioned to mutual manual stimulation. Orgasm with manual stimulation was more physically intense for Juan, although symbolically he preferred orgasm during intercourse. They accepted each other's erotic voice without it being a competition or performance.

Lydia felt more sexually satisfied than at any time in her life. She had come a long way and celebrated sexual vitality. Juan took pride in the success of this marriage. He did not think he could have a satisfying, secure, and sexual marriage and was immensely proud of achieving this. He attributes much of their success to Lydia believing in him. Juan enjoyed the emotional support of his son's family and Lydia's daughters. Juan was not just successful professionally and financially, he felt successful relationally and sexually.

Once a year, Lydia and Juan scheduled a three-day weekend at a cabin on a lake. They loved canoeing and hiking. The most important agenda was a check-in on the state of their marriage and marital sexuality. They focused on the balance of synchronous and asynchronous sexual experiences. With aging (Lydia was now 81 and Juan 76), asynchronous experiences were more common. They wanted to ensure that desire/pleasure/eroticism/satisfaction remained positive. Checking in about intimacy and sexuality was Lydia's domain—she had spent too much of her life dealing with marginal or dysfunctional sex. She looked forward to being sexual throughout the rest of her life. She was not willing to go back. Lydia's enthusiasm was contagious. She was Juan's intimate and erotic friend and cheerleader. Juan had always assumed that sex was better for him than his partner. He valued their equitable sexual relationship. He needed her sexual responsivity now in a manner he had not at the beginning of their relationship, and he liked it this way.

If there were emotional, relational, or sexual concerns the weekend at the cabin was the time to address them. Just as important was setting a new goal for the next year. They would not take sexuality for granted—a new sexual input kept their relationship alive. One year, Juan initiated a playful afterplay scenario using a finger game. Lydia initiated a multiple stimulation erotic scenario where she stood while Juan pleasured her using oral and manual stimulation while she manually stimulated him. The specifics of the sexual scenario are less important than being open to trying something new. Ideally you set two sexual goals each year. Security is good, but routine, totally predictable sex does not promote desire. Unpredictable sexual scenarios promote desire.

Lydia and Juan planned to be a sexual couple until age 85 and hopefully beyond. For that to be reality they needed to dialogue, putting thought and energy into their sexual relationship.

The Tyranny of Synchronous Sexual Demands

A common trap is the demand that all sex be synchronous. This is an especially easy trap for the Best Friend couple sexual style. With the emphasis on intimacy and mutuality, synchronous sex would seem to be the right fit, but it isn't. Enjoy synchronous experiences, but do not demand that all sex be synchronous. You end up either avoiding or arguing whose fault it is because you don't achieve this perfectionistic goal.

A large majority of encounters are positive, but 5–15% of sexual experiences are dissatisfying or dysfunctional. By its nature, sexual variability and flexibility increase with aging. The perfect is the enemy of the good. Demanding that all sex be synchronous is the enemy of sexual satisfaction. Unrealistic performance expectations undermine your sexual relationship.

The need for synchronous sex subverts initiation and frequency. Unless both partners are equally desirous, you wind up avoiding a sexual encounter. Sex becomes self-conscious, resulting in a low-sex marriage.

The answer to this dilemma is accepting the value of both asynchronous and synchronous sex. It is "both-and" not "either-or". Celebrate mutual, synchronous sex without it becoming a demand. Synchronous sex is great, just don't make it the only acceptable type of sex.

The Traps of Asynchronous Sex

We are strong advocates for asynchronous sex, but be aware of potential problems. The major trap is when the asynchronous scenario is at the expense of your partner or relationship. An example is if one partner finds a domination–submission scenario highly erotic (10), but the other finds it −3; this is not acceptable. If you find it a 2 this is fine. Be sure the asynchronous scenario is not negative for the partner. This is a bright red boundary. Violating this makes asynchronous sexuality destructive. Another example is if the scenario undermines your relationship by causing an emotional or sexual cut-off. For example, the traditional fellatio position of woman kneeling–man standing. This is erotic for many couples, although more for the man. However, if she feels coerced, humiliated, or that it's her duty to service him, this negates asynchronous sex.

The healthy asynchronous message is that the scenario is good for both partners and your relationship. For one partner the scenario is a 10 while for the other it is a 7 or 3. Asynchronous sex adds spice and vitality to your relationship (McCarthy & Oppliger, 2019). Sex has a variety of roles, meanings, and outcomes. Asynchronous sexuality encourages partners to take risks and maintain regular and frequent sexual connection. Asynchronous encounters allow you to engage in a range of sexual initiations for a range of motivations. Sometimes sex is intimate and pleasure-oriented, sometimes a tension reducer, sometimes a way to reconnect, sometimes selfish, sometimes playful, sometimes to spice up a dull day, sometimes to induce sleep, sometimes to give you energy to deal with a difficult parental or financial issue. Sometimes sex is spontaneous and other times planned.

The frequency of intercourse for young couples is three to 12 times a month. The average is a bit more than once a week (Laumann, Gagnon, Michael, & Michaels, 1994). For aging couples, especially those who accept GES and include sensual, playful, and erotic scenarios in addition to intercourse, a regular pattern of sexual connection is reinforced. Ideally there is sexual involvement at least twice a month and preferably twice a week or more. The majority of sexual encounters are asynchronous.

What is unhealthy is one partner feeling pressured with sex stuck in a mediocre or dissatisfying pattern. Contrary to traditional gender beliefs it is more likely the man who falls into a mediocre or disappointing sex pattern. He looks back at the "old days" when he was sexually dominant rather than enjoying sexual equity and variable, flexible couple sexuality in the present. Ideally, he embraces the new normal of responsive male sexual desire; variable, flexible sexual response; and subjective satisfaction rather than demanding flawless performance (McCarthy & McCarthy, 2012). He enjoys asynchronous sexuality, especially when he uses her sexual response as a cue to enhance his sexual responsivity. Rather than clinging to the old pattern, enjoy variable, flexible sexuality which includes intercourse and orgasm, but is not limited to that. Wise men accept asynchronous GES as first class. Your partner is your intimate and erotic ally who welcomes a variety of sexual experiences. Synchronous experiences usually involve intercourse. Accepting asynchronous experiences does not negate synchronous sex. Healthy couples accept both asynchronous and synchronous sexuality.

Exercise: Creating and Valuing Asynchronous and Synchronous Sexuality

Since it is more common with aging, let us begin with asynchronous sexual scenarios. Each partner creates two or three favorite asynchronous scenarios. This often involves intercourse but need not. Examples of asynchronous scenarios are:

1. Self-entrancement arousal where the receiving partner is pleasured to orgasm and the giving partner finds it a 5.

2. Both partners are equally involved in pleasuring. One stays at subjective arousal of 4 while the other's subjective arousal is 10.
3. You engage in intercourse where the woman is orgasmic, and the man is not. End the scenario in a warm, cuddly manner.
4. The man enjoys the scenario where his arousal is 8 before transitioning to intercourse. She enjoys the encounter at subjective arousal of 5.
5. You engage in self-entrancement arousal where she is multi-orgasmic, including self-stimulation. The experience is a 10 for her and a 7 for him.
6. The man initiates a role enactment arousal/eroticism scenario where his hands are tied so he can't stimulate her. She finds this a 6 while it is 10 for him.
7. They have a quickie in the car where he is orgasmic first. Afterward, she is orgasmic with oral stimulation. This experience is an 8 for him and a 10 for her.
8. They engage in a playful scenario which is a 3 for one and 7 for the other.
9. They have a mutual erotic scenario. He goes with the erotic flow to orgasm while she enjoys the feelings and sensations at 8.
10. She initiates a "me focused" date beginning with a bath and glass of wine. They engage in partner interaction sensual and playful touching. They transition to self-entrancement arousal where she lets go and is multi-orgasmic. A 10 for her and a 6 for him.

The key for asynchronous scenarios is both feel good, although it is more satisfying for one partner.

The second phase of this exercise focuses on creating synchronous sexual scenarios. You cannot demand synchronous sex, nor is it a performance goal. If the experience does not turn out to be synchronous, enjoy asynchronous sexuality. In synchronous scenarios the intention is both partners experience high levels of desire/pleasure/eroticism/satisfaction.

1. Begin with a scenario where you anticipate being sexual and engage in sensual and playful touch to facilitate responsive

desire; transition to erotic stimulation when subjective arousal is 6; engage in multiple stimulation before intercourse; transition to intercourse when subjective arousal is 8 or 9 with her guiding intromission; intercourse in the woman on top position using long, slow thrusting; both partners giving and receiving multiple stimulation during intercourse including private erotic fantasies; experiencing orgasm during intercourse; and engaging in intimate afterplay to enhance satisfaction.

2. Agree on a mutual erotic date with a prohibition on intercourse. Begin with sensual touch, transition to playful touching, engage in manual and oral stimulation to erotic flow, each partner is orgasmic in your preferred manner (manual, oral, or rubbing stimulation). Enjoy a quiet, meaningful afterplay.
3. Begin with playful, seductive touch which is pleasurable for both partners. Switch to mutual erotic touch, focusing on the woman's arousal and orgasm before intercourse. Transition to intercourse where you enjoy short, rapid thrusting in the man-on-top position. Afterplay is mutual and satisfying.
4. Enjoy a sensual date using self-entrancement arousal and taking turns. Share a glass of wine as you engage with sensual touching. There is no expectation of intercourse or orgasm. The level of mutual pleasure is 3. Afterplay is a continuation of warm and cuddly touching and emotional connection.
5. For a couple who no longer have intercourse, create a scenario to share eroticism and orgasm, using partner interaction arousal. Rather than beginning in a sensual manner, begin with a playful scenario involving music and dancing. Seductively take your partner's clothes off. Don't begin genital stimulation until subjective arousal is 8. Use oral stimulation for her orgasm while he is orgasmic with oral stimulation while actively thrusting. Lie and hold, acknowledging the vitality of your sexual relationship.

This exercise encourages you to create and enjoy a range of asynchronous and synchronous scenarios. Celebrate the roles, meanings, and outcomes of couple sexuality with aging.

Summary

Both synchronous and asynchronous sexual experiences are integral to couple sexuality with aging. Although the best sex is mutual and synchronous, asynchronous sexuality is the norm with aging. This is not a loss. It is a challenge—celebrate the range of sexual roles, meanings, and outcomes. As long as asynchronous sexuality is not at the expense of your partner or relationship it reinforces desire. With aging you need each other in a way you didn't 20 years before. This creates resilient sexual desire and satisfaction.

Rather than focus on individual sex performance, celebrate GES as a couple experience. Celebrate mutual, synchronous sex (whether or not it involves intercourse). The key to synchronous sex is the mutual experience of desire/pleasure/eroticism/satisfaction. In addition, celebrate asynchronous sex. This includes accepting that sexuality does not require intercourse or orgasm. With aging, asynchronous sexuality is often better for the woman. The man embraces the new model of variable, flexible GES.

Both asynchronous and synchronous scenarios support couple sexuality with aging. Acceptance and pleasure facilitate sexual satisfaction.

10

A PILL CAN'T DO IT ALL: A PSYCHOBIOSOCIAL APPROACH TO SEX

The drug companies lie to men (and women) about sex. They promise that a stand-alone medical intervention (medications, testosterone, or injections) will cure any sex problem. In the psychobiosocial model of understanding, assessing, and treating sex problems, you are urged to use all your psychological, biomedical, and social/relational resources to promote sexual desire and function. The couple comprehensive approach will help you be sexual in your 60s, 70s, and 80s. This includes attending to health and medical factors. Anything that is good for your physical body is good for your sexual body. The good news is there is no illness or disability which stops you from being sexual. The bad news is that many couples stop sex after 60. The chief cause is male sex dysfunction, especially erectile dysfunction (ED). We advocate for the strategies of responsive sexual desire for both women and men and for Good Enough Sex (GES).

Confront the stand-alone biomedical model and replace it with the couple psychobiosocial model for understanding and addressing sexual problems (Metz, Epstein, & McCarthy, 2017). When you use medical interventions (pills, creams, injections, testosterone, dilators, vibrators), the intervention needs to be integrated into your couple sexual style of intimacy, pleasuring, and eroticism. Just as important is to change your definition of sex to include sensual, playful, and erotic scenarios in addition to intercourse. Develop positive, realistic expectations based on the GES model rather than expect perfect individual performance. A pill or other medical intervention cannot do it all sexually. Rather than hoping for a stand-alone intervention, use all your resources to promote sexuality with aging. The most important guidelines are that the essence of sexuality is giving and receiving pleasure-oriented touching and being an intimate sexual team.

The individual biomedical approach to sex does not work with aging. The couple psychobiosocial model focused on desire/pleasure/eroticism/satisfaction is a good fit. An important guideline is to accept the new normal. Value broad-based sexuality which supports variable, flexible GES.

Couple Consultation with a Primary Care Physician or Specialist

A strong recommendation is to schedule a couple consultation with your physician rather than follow the routine of one partner going alone and returning with a prescription. Physicians are used to seeing patients alone. If you attend as a couple it will bring out the best in the doctor. This is especially true when dealing with sexual problems. Physicians want to help, but are not well trained in sexual medicine so adopt a "don't ask" approach. They say they don't have the time or expertise to deal with a complex problem like sexuality, especially sex and aging.

When you request a consultation as a couple be clear you are not asking the doctor to be a sex therapist. You are asking for biomedical resources to enhance sexual desire and function. For example, a way to motivate a spouse to stop smoking is awareness that smoking is bad for his penis or her vulva because it subverts vascular function. Another example is improved sleep habits—poor sleep causes low sexual desire. In consulting a specialist (cardiologist for heart problems, endocrinologist for diabetes, oncologist for cancer, pain specialist for back problems, psychiatrist for depression), you are promoting a sophisticated perspective on the sex problem rather than expecting a medication to solve it. Addressing biomedical factors is necessary, but not sufficient. Changing attitudes, behaviors, and emotions is as important as receiving a prescription. Change in medications or dosage can make a significant difference. An example is anti-depressant medication. Switch to an anti-depressant with fewer side-effects. If you prefer being sexual at night take your medication in the morning so there are fewer side-effects when you have sex. Another example is a couple consultation with the oncologist—cancer affects the spouse as well as the person with cancer. Do you utilize touching and sexuality as a way to reinforce your relationship as you cope with cancer? Fatigue interferes with sexual desire and response. When do you feel most awake and receptive to touch? If breast cancer, how do you feel about touching the infected vs, non-infected breast? How can you support each other as you deal with cancer?

Knowledge is power. Awareness of illness, disability, and biomedical factors is crucial. Utilize all your resources, including biomedical resources, to improve couple sexuality. What is not helpful is to look to a medication or medical intervention as a stand-alone resource to solve the problem. Integrate the medical intervention into your couple sexual style of intimacy, pleasuring, and eroticism (Perelman, 2009). The illness/disability is a couple challenge. Accept the new normal, but do not give it control over your sexuality.

The medical expert is your consultant on how to address the sexual health problem rather than feel controlled by it. The physician cannot provide a cure but can help you understand and deal with the illness and its sexual implications. Consulting the physician as a couple makes it less likely that the physician will minimize the problem or just write a prescription. The physician can provide guidance about medical, medication, and behavioral health recommendations so that negative sexual effects are minimized.

A growing trend in medicine is to implement the biopsychosocial (we prefer the term psychobiosocial) model of assessment and treatment to replace the narrow biomedical model. This is even more relevant when dealing with aging. Aging isn't primarily about physical loss and illness. Aging is about meeting your challenges and utilizing psychological, biomedical, and relational resources. A gerontologist (an important medical sub-specialty) is most likely to embrace the comprehensive psychobiosocial approach to understanding and treatment. Physicians can direct patients to reliable resources and away from overpromising companies who recommend scientifically unproven supplements and biomedical cures.

The Most Common Problem—Erectile Dysfunction (ED)

With the introduction of Viagra in 1998, drug company ads reinforced the public expectation that the "little blue pill" was the cure for ED. The good news is that Cialis and Viagra are valuable resources to treat ED. The bad news is that Viagra has caused more non-sexual relationships than ever. This is because of perfectionistic expectations (a return to the totally predictable erections of your 20s). No one explains to the man and couple how to integrate the medication into your couple sexual style. Almost no man obtains the totally reliable erection portrayed in the ads. Based on the perfect performance criterion almost all men are "Viagra failures". A realistic expectation is you will have an erection sufficient for intercourse 65–85% of the time (Kalogeropoulos & Larouche, 2020). A comprehensive couple approach is the basis for the GES model (Metz & McCarthy, 2004).

GES advocates an approach which promotes sexual confidence. It's very different than what you are promised by the drug companies. The core issue is whether medication can be a stand-alone intervention for ED. Key to regaining erectile comfort and confidence is the couple work together to promote pleasure, arousal, and erotic flow. Especially with aging, you need to be an intimate sexual team. Viagra can't do it all. The most violated guideline is to not transition to intercourse until you feel (subjectively and objectively) into erotic flow-arousal of 8 or at least 7. Instead, as soon as you get an erection (subjective arousal 4–5) you rush to intercourse driven by fear of losing your erection. Rather than an integrative couple approach, sex becomes an individual pass–fail erection test. You are always one failed intercourse from feeling like a "sexual failure". The fatal flaw of this approach to ED is unrealistic performance demands for a stand-alone intervention. This is true for almost all medical interventions for men (and women). The medical intervention needs to be integrated into your couple sexual style and be congruent with GES expectations. Healthy sexuality is anti-perfectionistic.

The most important learning is to approach sexuality as an intimate sexual team focused on sharing pleasure. The more you invest yourself in a medication, injection, or testosterone as a stand-alone cure for ED (or low desire), the more likely you will be frustrated, embarrassed, and eventually give up sex. You are embarrassed and avoid sex. You feel embarrassed that the medical cure did not work for you. You stop sex because you feel defeated that a pill which is supposed to cure all men is a failure for you. From our perspective, this disappointment and avoidance is to be expected. You (and your partner) asked the medication to do more than it could do. In common medical problems (high blood pressure, diabetes, obesity) the medical intervention needs to be combined with behavioral changes including exercise, sleep, and eating patterns, stopping smoking, and reducing alcohol. Additional psychological and relational changes are helpful in resolving sexual problems. Perhaps the most important change involves attitudes and expectations. Rather than total failure or total success, you adopt a positive, realistic model of change, especially altering sexual expectations. An individualized, multi-dimensional approach to sexual change empowers you to stay with the process rather than give up.

The stand-alone medication approach sets you up for failure. Use all your psychological, biomedical, and social/relational resources to promote meaningful change. Equally important is motivation to maintain sexual gains.

The majority of couples over age 60 are dealing with medical problems and taking medications. This makes it likely that you will experience sexual changes. Change does not mean sex dysfunction or giving up sex. Remember, desire and satisfaction are the core dimensions of couple sexuality.

Clarissa and Prem

Sexuality was a challenge for 78-year-old Clarissa and 74-year-old Prem. This was Prem's first marriage and Clarissa's third. They had two adult children from their marriage and three adult children from Clarissa's prior marriages. In addition, they had seven grandchildren who they enjoyed and were valued grandparents. Clarissa and Prem had an exceptionally good quality of life even though their physical health was only fair. A particular vulnerability was sexual health.

For years Clarissa used a vaginal lubricant and a moisturizer to deal with vaginal dryness. She practiced mindfulness on a regular basis which enhanced sexual awareness and responsivity. In addition, she consulted a female physical therapist with a specialty in pelvic muscle function. Previously Clarissa had been orgasmic with manual and intercourse stimulation, but now was most responsive to manual stimulation. This involved vulva and clitoral stimulation with occasional use of intra-vaginal finger stimulation. Prem enjoyed her sexual responsivity which enhanced his desire and arousal. Prem's physical health was better than Clarissa's, but his sexual health was tenuous. For the past ten years, Prem had used Viagra an hour before a sexual encounter. In over 85% of experiences he had an erection sufficient for intercourse. When sex did not flow to intercourse, they engaged in mutual manual stimulation to orgasm. Clarissa accepted this, but Prem became frustrated about his sex function. He felt that over time Viagra had become less effective. After seeing an ad on sports tv he called for an individual appointment at a men's sexual health clinic which offered a refund if he wasn't completely satisfied. Prem did not like the high cost of the initial consultation, but was pleased there were only two appointments. The first involved a number of medical tests and in the second he received a prescription for testosterone enhancement and a physician's assistant showed him how to do penile injections. Prem returned home feeling sexually confident that with higher testosterone and reliable erections he would feel like a "real man". His optimism and enthusiasm lasted one week. Clarissa was glad he had a firm erection when he left the bathroom, but he rushed intercourse before she had a chance to utilize the vaginal cream. His rapid thrusting resulted in vaginal pain. Prem had difficulty reaching orgasm. Although he maintained a firm erection, he did not feel "turned-on"—subjective arousal was low. When he finally did ejaculate, it was a relief rather than a pleasurable feeling. Clarissa felt confused and alienated. His sexual solution negated her sexual feelings. She felt he was working around her rather than with her. She wanted to understand what was happening, but Prem was defensive and avoided a discussion.

Two days later he told her about the men's sexual health clinic and using penile injections. Clarissa understood his desire for a firm erection but asked why he did the injection by himself in the bathroom. His response was that he felt embarrassed. She urged him to engage with her and to do the injection while she caressed him.

For the next month, Prem and Clarissa experimented with different ways to integrate the injection into their couple sexual style. Sometimes she would do the injection, sometimes he would. Sometimes they would engage in touching before the injection and other times touching after the injection. Clarissa used her vaginal lubricant before intromission. Usually, Clarissa would be orgasmic before intercourse.

At the end of the month, they had a conversation sitting in their living room with a glass of wine. Clarissa said that as long as Prem enjoyed intercourse she was fine with the penile injection. However, Prem admitted he was disappointed with the injection. It felt awkward rather than pleasurable. Although it resulted in a firm erection, it was not a "magic" solution. He enjoyed the sexual experience more when he took a pro-erection medication. As a couple, they consulted his internist who recommended Prem take a daily low dose Cialis. In the clinician's clinical experience this was a valuable strategy. It allowed Prem and Clarissa to initiate sex when they liked. The encounter would flow to intercourse most of the time. When it didn't, the internist asked Clarissa how she felt about manual sexuality. Clarissa was affirmative. She noted that this would be better than the penile injection for her, but worried it would be disappointing for Prem. The internist noted in a joking manner that this was the traditional male–female split. The man wanted sex certainty (reliable erection and intercourse) while the woman wanted sex to be pleasurable and satisfying.

A daily low dose Cialis pill reduces anticipatory anxiety but does not guarantee sex function. Rather than feel "ganged up on" Prem felt permission to do what he really wanted. He did not like penile injections. It was not the stand-alone intervention he had been promised at the men's clinic. In addition, testosterone enhancement had a number of side-effects—the most disruptive was it interfered with sleep and caused heightened irritability. The internist found Prem's testosterone level was in the normal range. She recommended he stop testosterone. Testosterone is more effective and safer as an injection rather than orally. Prem had enough of injections and was glad to stop both testosterone and penile injections.

Prem and Clarissa left the consultation feeling more informed and optimistic. Clarissa had made her preferences clear—she affirmed variable, flexible couple sexuality. She appreciated Prem's preference for intercourse but wanted him to accept her satisfaction with erotic sexuality. Being orgasmic with manual stimulation was easier and more satisfying. Prem finally got that message. He accepted that although Cialis was a good intervention, it was not a stand-alone, guaranteed approach to erection and intercourse. Clarissa did not need intercourse to feel good about a sexual encounter. Prem would have loved to find a comfortable medical intervention which resulted in predictable erection and intercourse. He realized genital stimulation and Cialis facilitated better, but not perfect, erection and intercourse. He was a "wise" man who accepted what his wife and internist said about GES. Do not cling to the traditional male hope for a stand-alone medical intervention for guaranteed erections.

Clarissa's enthusiasm for GES won Prem over. He felt better about a daily Cialis pill. Prem took pride in "beating the odds" and enjoying pleasure-oriented couple sexuality in his 70s and 80s.

Valuing the Psychobiosocial Approach Rather than a Stand-Alone Biomedical Intervention

The biomedical model advocates a stand-alone intervention to cure a sex problem. The psychobiosocial model advocates using all your psychological, biomedical, and social/relational resources to enhance couple sexuality. You cannot ask a medicine to do it all nor guarantee a perfect result. Changing health behaviors (better sleep, exercise, and eating habits, stopping smoking, and reducing or stopping drinking) is important for your sexual health. Psychological and relational factors are integral to couple sexuality. Accepting GES is core to the change process. It is crucial to promote sexual health. Perhaps the most important factor is embracing variable, flexible, sexual expression. A scenario of responsive sexual desire, receptivity to pleasurable touching, building arousal and eroticism, transitioning to intercourse at high levels of subjective arousal, and erotic flow leading to orgasm is wonderful. However, that is not the typical scenario. Aging sexual response is variable and less predictable. Sex is more likely to be asynchronous and is vulnerable to disruption. Relationally, you need each other as intimate and erotic allies in a manner you didn't 20 years earlier. Asking a stand-alone medication to be a substitute for sexual flexibility is asking too much. The traditional arousal, intercourse, and orgasm approach will not work every time. Sometimes a sensual or erotic scenario is a better alternative. Other times the sexual experience is asynchronous, particularly good for one partner while okay for the other. For both men and women, orgasm becomes less reliable. Sometimes the medical intervention is seamless and successful; other times it provides a weak sexual response. The psychobiosocial approach of acceptance rather than demand all sex be perfect is a better fit. Functional or dysfunctional sex is too simplistic to describe the roles, meanings, and outcomes of couple sexuality with aging. A key to sex after 60 is acceptance of variable, flexible sexuality. Hoping for a stand-alone medical intervention compounds the problem. Turn toward your partner and accept your sexual experiences. This is a sign of healthy couple sexuality.

Exercise: Confronting the Biomedical Stand-Alone Model

The biomedical model for sex problems is much more evident among men and male physicians. This exercise is more impactful when done as a couple. Start by listing all the possible biomedical interventions for your sex problem(s). For men this would include Viagra, Cialis, testosterone, penile injections, penile pumps, desensitizing cream for PE, anti-anxiety medication, over-the-counter sexual enhancement pills. For women biomedical interventions include injections or medications to enhance desire, a vibrator, testosterone, vaginal lubricants, and over-the-counter sexual enhancement pills or creams. Would these be beneficial for you and/or your partner to promote sexual confidence and function? If so, how would you implement the intervention? A core issue is whether you expect the medical intervention to work as a stand-alone solution to the sex problem. How can you integrate the biomedical intervention into your couple sexual style?

Rather than falling into the simplistic trap of the intervention as a stand-alone solution to all sex problems, be a healthy couple and adopt the psychobiosocial approach. Whether a medication, a behavioral addition like a vibrator or cream, or a change in health behavior like an improved sleeping pattern, what is an efficacious approach to promote desire/pleasure/eroticism/satisfaction? For example, how to utilize a vaginal lubricant. Are you more comfortable doing this by yourself or do you want your partner to use the lubricant as part of pleasuring? What level of subjective arousal facilitates the efficacy of the lubricant? Do you approach sexual pain as a couple issue and work together to enhance sexual comfort and confidence?

An example of the importance of integrating a medication is the decision to use Viagra or Cialis. A man who likes structure or is a procrastinator will do better with Viagra because it provides a specific window of opportunity (1–4 hours) in which to initiate sex. Men (and women) who value spontaneity and unpredictability find Cialis a better fit because it provides a 30-minute–30-hour window of opportunity. What is the right fit for you personally and as a couple? Does the medical intervention facilitate your sexual function and confidence? It is not a "magic pill", but part of a comprehensive psychobiosocial approach to maintaining erectile confidence. Can you accept a non-perfectionistic approach to erection and aging? Can you integrate the medication with GES guidelines?

Consider three issues in this exercise: (1) What biomedical intervention is most helpful in facilitating desire/pleasure/eroticism/satisfaction? (2) How to integrate this intervention into your couple sexual style of intimacy, pleasuring, and eroticism? (3) How to develop positive, realistic sexual expectations rather than demand perfect sex performance?

Adopting the Psychobiosocial Model for Sexuality and Aging

It is easier to give up the hope for a stand-alone medical answer to a sex problem when you adopt a better strategy. Acceptance of the psychobiosocial model for understanding and change is that strategy. For sexuality and aging it is crucial to affirm the new normal and not compare it to young adult sex. Utilize all your psychological, biomedical, and social/relational resources to promote couple sexuality. Positive learnings about couple sexuality come to fruition with aging. The core concepts are to focus on pleasure-oriented touching and value the range of sexual roles, meanings, and outcomes. Viewing sex as an individual intercourse test and looking to a stand-alone medical intervention to promote performance is self-defeating. This results in a no-sex or low-sex relationship. Embrace the variability and flexibility of couple sexuality. The psychobiosocial model gives you a solid foundation for sexuality with aging.

Summary

The drug and medical companies hate this chapter, but aging couples celebrate these guidelines. Sexuality is more human and genuine with aging. Find the right fit of resources and interventions to promote desire/pleasure/eroticism/satisfaction. Do not accept simplistic, overpromising biomedical claims. Medications and medical interventions are helpful resources, but don't be seduced by promises of "miracle cures". An advantage of biomedical resources is to promote sexual expectations. This has been labeled the "placebo effect". Placebo facilitates attitudinal change and openness which is an important resource when combined with psychological, biomedical, and social/relational resources. The most important factors are turning toward your partner as your intimate and erotic ally and embracing variable, flexible couple sexuality. The message is to use all your personal and couple resources. Do not expect a biomedical intervention to do it all.

11

SEXUALLY, ONE SIZE NEVER FITS ALL: DIFFERENCES AND DIVERSITY

An important cultural change is the acceptance of sexual diversity. Sexually, one size never fits all. We respect differences and diversity whether gay or lesbian couples, non-binary individuals, atypical sexual expression, couples who practice BDSM (bondage/discipline, sadomasochism), gender fluidity, and a variety of relational and sexual values.

You have a right to sexual pleasure whether your values are traditional or non-traditional. Whether 75 or 25, live your life in a manner which expresses your values and realities. This is not a negation of traditional couples or their values. The essence of mainstream values is honoring a satisfying, secure, and sexual marriage. Monogamy and children are part of mainstream values. There is no reason for traditional couples to feel threatened or negated by gay couples, divorced or widowed people, lifelong single people, couples who practice polyamory, asexual individuals, swinging couples, or those with a "kinky" arousal pattern. There are two core concepts. First, you have the right to express your "authentic sexual self". Second, sexual minorities do not negate mainstream couple sexuality. Sexuality is not a "zero-sum" game. Alternative ways to express sexuality are not a threat to traditional couples. Each person has a right to their sexual preferences and values. Affirm that one size does not fit all; accept sexual complexity and diversity. As long as sexual expression is among adults (not involving children), voluntary (nor forced or coerced), private (not sexual in public), and is not destructive for either partner (not manipulative or have a hidden agenda), it is in the normal range of sexual expression.

There are people with traditional sexual values (prioritize your relationship and a genuine commitment to monogamy) who are judgmental about alternative sexualities whether gay couples, swinging, sexual friendships, polyamory, fetish sexual expression, BDSM, or consensual non-monogamy. The misperception is that sexual health professionals advocate non-traditional sexuality and view mainstream sexuality as inhibited and repressive. This is nonsense. Every individual and every couple has the right to sexual health. The challenge is to find the right fit for your emotions, behaviors, and values. It is not mainstream vs. non-traditional. It is what is healthy for you psychologically, relationally, and sexually. Sexual orientation provides a good example. The great majority of individuals and couples are heterosexual. This means their genuine emotional attachment and genuine erotic expression is with someone of the opposite gender. The term "heteronormative" is descriptive, not judgmental. The negative use of heteronormative is that heterosexuality is the only acceptable sexual orientation or that it's the optimal sexual orientation. A scientifically accurate and culturally healthy approach is to determine your authentic sexual self and live your sexual life in a positive manner. For gay (or lesbian) individuals, being gay is optimal. You are a first-class person and a first-class couple.

There is scientific support for at least four sexual orientations—heterosexual, homosexual, bisexual+, and asexual (Anderson, 2017). Sexual orientation means much more than who you fantasize about and who you have sex with. Sexual orientation is the integration of genuine emotional bonding and genuine erotic expression. Sexual orientation signifies the essence of you as a sexual person.

Gay, Lesbian, Asexual, and Bisexual+

There are challenges for gay, lesbian, and bisexual+ individuals and couples. The core issue is to live in a healthy manner so that sexuality has a positive 15–20% role in your life and relationship. For some aging gay people, this has been true for over 50 years, but for most accepting your sexual orientation has been a struggle for many years if not your entire life. Many, especially gay men, had a "secret sexual life" for years. You cannot compensate for the past, but you owe it to yourself to lead a healthy, integrated sexual life now. Accept that you are a first-class gay man (or lesbian woman) who deserves sexual pleasure.

Asexuality is a genuine sexual orientation involving less than 2% of adult women and less than 1% of adult men. Asexuality is a lifelong characteristic—you do not value sexual touch or sexual pleasure (Brotto, Yule, & Gorzalka, 2015). Traditionally, asexual people were unaware and likely to marry and have children, but sex was not a valued part of life. The challenge is acceptance that asexuality is who you are without blaming or shaming. In many ways, asexuality is easier to accept with aging. A core issue facing gay men is acceptance. In your generation, homosexuality was viewed as deviant and unacceptable. The good news in 2021 is that being gay is recognized as normal. For you being gay is not just acceptable it is optimal. This is a crucial, liberating message for all gay men, but is especially challenging for the aging gay man in a heterosexual marriage. You married with the hope that a loving marriage would "cure" your sexual orientation. Sexual orientation is "hard-wired", not a lifestyle choice. You don't cure sexual orientation. You don't need a wife to justify your life or provide social acceptance. The healthy approach (whether at age 70 or 20) is to accept that your authentic sexual self is gay. You cannot expect your spouse to accept this unless you are a proud gay man. That does not mean rejecting your past life, your spouse, or your family. It means being a proud gay man in the present. Make a "wise" couple decision. The most common decision for aging couples is to maintain the marriage, treat each other with empathy and respect, be an affectionate couple, and accept sexual friendships with gay men. Of course, many couples choose a "good divorce". Others stay legally married (often for financial or family reasons), but live separately. Still others maintain a committed marriage, including sexual involvement.

The core guideline is one size never fits all. Decide on the right fit for you (and your spouse) based on your values and realities. What you cannot do is feel shameful about being gay.

Many gay men have lived part (or all) of their lives in a secretive manner. An advantage of aging is it gives you the opportunity to be your authentic sexual self. Ideally, you would accept being gay as an adolescent or young adult, but it's never too late—even after age 70.

Traditionally, the gay community was not an advocate for aging gay men. In the "bad old days" older men were expected to settle for a manipulative sexual relationship with a younger man. The theme was that gay sex was about youth, perfect bodies, taking risks, illicitness, eroticism, and breaking boundaries. Gay sex was supposed to be new and hot. Older gay men were not valued. What a destructive, unscientific approach. You deserve to enjoy sexuality and your sexual relationship. Your challenge is to live your psychological, relational, and sexual life in a first-class manner.

Many gay couples are of similar age, others have significant age differences. A core issue is whether you view the relationship as a marriage (life partnership), a lover relationship, or a sexual friendship. What is your level of commitment and what are your relational expectations? Is each partner committed to desire/pleasure/eroticism/satisfaction? Traditionally, gay relationships focused on eroticism, downplaying intimacy and pleasuring. The majority of gay couples integrate intimacy, pleasuring, and eroticism. A critical factor is whether you have a monogamy agreement, a "monogamish" approach, or value consensual nonmonogamy. Creating a clear agreement is valuable. You want sexuality to have a 15–20% role in your life and relationship in your 60s, 70s, and 80s. To make this guideline meaningful you need to confront the stereotypes of gay sexuality. Make a wise decision based on your values and relationship. Do not fall into the trap of a contingent self-esteem or a contingent relationship. Be a proud gay man who affirms that being gay is optimal for you. Value a first-class relationship.

Lesbian Couples

The challenges for lesbian women and relationships are different. Lesbian couples are psychologically and relationally healthier than male couples, especially with regard to greater security. On many measures, lesbian couples are more satisfied than heterosexual couples. A core challenge for lesbian couples is to integrate sexuality generally and eroticism specifically. After the limerence phase, you are in danger of losing your "sexual voice" and settling for a low-sex or no-sex relationship. In terms of the desire/pleasure/eroticism/satisfaction mantra, the strength of lesbian couples is pleasure and satisfaction. Vulnerabilities are desire and eroticism. Emphasize "responsive sexual desire" and reinforce your "erotic voice". Integrated eroticism is integral to lesbian sexuality. A particularly valuable strategy is to develop "your", "her", and "our" bridges to sexual desire. Valuing sensual, playful, and erotic touch is part of your relationship. Manual, oral, and rubbing stimulation are the most common forms of sexual expression. Some couples utilize insertive sex whether with fingers, a dildo, or other mechanisms while others do not value insertive sex. What is right for you?

A common vulnerability (trap) for lesbian couples is putting so much emphasis on intimacy that you "de-eroticize" your partner and relationship. The challenge for couples—married or partnered—is to find the right balance of intimacy and eroticism. Your relationship meets needs for intimacy and pleasure as well as for playfulness, eroticism, and vitality. A second vulnerability is to put so much emphasis on mutuality that you don't initiate or take sexual risks. This results in a low-sex relationship. It is easier to hang out and cuddle rather than take the risk and initiate a sexual encounter. A core strategy is to affirm the value of asynchronous sexuality (positive, but better for one partner). Overemphasis on mutual sexual experiences can thwart sexual initiation and risk-taking. Mutuality is good, but don't allow it to become the "tyranny of mutuality". Although synchronous sex is ideal (both partners experience high levels of desire/pleasure/eroticism/satisfaction), most sexual encounters are asynchronous. Focus on sexual initiation and engagement rather than sex performance. A key is freedom to welcome and integrate asynchronous sexuality. Asynchronous sex is positive as long as it's not at the expense of the partner or relationship.

Bisexual+ Individuals and Couples

Bisexual+ has always existed but is only now being recognized with a new label (it had been called pansexual or bisexual). Bisexual+ applies to women and men, and involves a genuine emotional and sexual bond with both genders. Bisexual+ is more common among women. There are more women who identify as bisexual+ than lesbian. Traditionally, gay men have derided bisexual men as not having the courage to accept being gay. Scientifically, that is wrong. Bisexual+ is a genuine sexual orientation. Bisexual+ does not mean 50–50, but that you have a genuine emotional attachment and genuine sexual charge with both men and women.

The challenge for bisexual+ is to define for yourself what this means psychologically, relationally, and sexually. A core issue is whether both partners identify as bisexual+. Often, one partner identifies as straight or gay. You need to clarify what bisexual+ means in your life and relationship. Many couples identified as a traditional heterosexual couple, and one partner had a secret sexual life. For other couples, the bisexual+ commitment came out over time. These are complicated issues that need to be explored in an honest, non-blaming manner. What is your emotional and sexual reality as a bisexual+ couple? For example, it is important to have a clear consensual non-monogamy agreement to ensure that sexuality has a positive rather than destabilizing role. Bisexual+ individuals and couples deserve healthy sexuality. It isn't enough to say that bisexual+ is normal, take pride in your authentic sexual self and relationship.

Claiming Your Atypical Sexual Voice

The majority of couples value intimate, interactive sexuality. Some couples have an atypical (variant or kinky) sexual arousal/eroticism pattern. This involves role enactment arousal/eroticism. There are multiple patterns, but the most common are a fetish arousal, a BDSM scenario, or sexual expression while crossdressed. As long as the atypical sexual expression is among adults, in private, not forced or coercive, not manipulative, it is in the normal range. This is your preferred sexual expression.

For many couples, the atypical sexual pattern has existed throughout your relationship (whether for two or 42 years). For other couples it is a recently added dimension. An example is the man has an erotic arousal to women's open sandals but did not introduce this into couple sexuality until age 62. Another example is a couple who focused on partner interaction arousal until you developed erectile anxiety. The woman introduced a BDSM scenario featuring you being tied to the bed and receiving erotic stimulation.

The clinical belief was that kinky (variant or atypical) arousal was a symbol of sexual trauma or an obsessive-compulsive disorder. The assumption was that kink arousal is caused by psychological problems. Do not assume that kink is problematic. For most, kink arousal is a strong sexual preference which is highly erotic for the person (usually the man). The question is whether it can be integrated into your couple sexual style. Usually the kink experience is asynchronous—better for the partner with the kink. Using a 10-point scale of subjective arousal, the kink scenario is a 10 for you—hopefully a 7, 4 or at least a 1 for your partner. Kink sexuality is used by straight and gay couples, married and partnered couples, and by women as well as men.

Gender Fluidity

Most in your generation grew up with clear, rigid socialization regarding what men did and what women did. What it meant to be a man was totally different than what it meant to be a woman. An advantage of sexuality and aging is greater freedom and less rigidity regarding gender roles. In your grandchildren's generation gender roles are more flexible. You have freedom to express yourself. This includes that it is healthy for men to value intimacy and pleasuring and women to value eroticism and intercourse.

For some aging people rigid sexual roles never fit. An example is transgender people. More commonly, those who identify as gender fluid or non-binary. This is an example that sexually one size never fits all. People have a right to their authentic sexual self, including gender expression. The culture is healthier with gender flexibility and acceptance rather than rigid, oppressive roles enforced by shame and fear of ostracism. Ideally, friends and family are supportive and accepting of gender fluidity.

In couples where there is conflict about atypical sexuality or gender fluidity you benefit from consulting a therapist with a specialty in these issues. Guidelines for choosing a sex, couple, or individual therapist are in Appendix A. Consult a therapist whose approach and values are the right fit for you.

Jennifer and Stacey

Jennifer, who is 72, and 66-year-old Stacey are a lesbian couple in a 19-year relationship. Jennifer left a 24-year heterosexual marriage when she accepted that her authentic sexual self was lesbian rather than heterosexual. Her young adult children, especially her college daughter who planned to be a mental health counselor, tried to convince Jennifer that she was bisexual and should stay married. The decision to divorce was not easy, but eventually they had a good divorce. She wished her ex-husband well. Jennifer told him he deserved a relationship with a heterosexual woman. Jennifer was sad but relieved after the divorce.

Jennifer enjoyed being married and hoped to develop a life partnership. She wanted to be sure this would be a satisfying, secure, and sexual relationship. Jennifer found the lesbian community and dating more welcoming than experiences with heterosexual dating. Jennifer was not expecting a limerence relationship so was very surprised when she fell in love with Stacey.

Stacey's sexual history was quite different. Stacey came out at age 18 and had always valued intimacy, pleasuring, and eroticism with a woman. Stacey viewed herself as pro-sexual and pro-eroticism. Her relationships lasted two to four years. She did not expect to create a life partnership until she began dating Jennifer. Stacey felt Jennifer was the kindest, most empathic woman she had ever been with. However, from the beginning eroticism was the weak link. Stacey hated the concept of "lesbian bed death". She has been upset when sexual desire and frequency weakened as a relationship lengthened. This was the first relationship Stacey had been in where sexuality did not have an erotic charge at the beginning. Rather than withdrawing, Stacey asked Jennifer to attend couple sex therapy with a lesbian sex therapist. Jennifer welcomed the opportunity to explore sexuality and create a couple sexual style.

Jennifer and Stacey found sex therapy a challenge. They explored psychological, family, relational, social, and sexual factors which facilitated desire and those which inhibited desire. They learned a great deal about themselves, each other, and the challenges of an intimate sexual relationship. Their vulnerabilities were very different. Stacey was used to desire and response being easy rather than exploring the nuances and complexity of desire. The vulnerability for Jennifer was she did not own her "erotic voice", specifically incorporating atypical erotic scenarios. Jennifer found masturbation easier than couple sex (with a woman or a man). Masturbation gave her freedom to utilize erotic materials and fantasies. Jennifer was shy about her arousal/erotic pattern. She went along with her partner's erotic scenarios rather than introducing her own. Stacey valued partner interaction arousal and enjoyed a range of pleasuring and erotic scenarios. She assumed this would be true of Jennifer, but it wasn't. Jennifer enjoyed giving and receiving sensual and playful touch to build responsive sexual desire. For Stacey eroticism involved self-entrancement arousal using specific erotic stimuli. Over a number of therapy sessions and engaging in psychosexual skill exercises, Jennifer's arousal/eroticism pattern became clear. Jennifer had a strong preference for being the giving partner first—Stacey experienced multi-orgasmic response with oral stimulation. This gave Jennifer permission to be the receiving partner. Stacey bound Jennifer's hands with silk ropes. Stacey provided oral breast stimulation and manual clitoral stimulation. When subjective arousal was 8–9, Jennifer's erotic pattern was one intense orgasm with manual stimulation. Afterplay was an essential component in Jennifer's scenario. Afterplay was warm and cuddly leading to a 20–30-minute nap. Stacey had discovered a hidden part of Jennifer. Although their erotic preferences were different, they affirmed the importance of desire/pleasure/eroticism/satisfaction.

A major breakthrough occurred when Jennifer masturbated in front of Stacey. Jennifer sharing her techniques for self-stimulation, use of bondage, and the strength of her orgasmic response provided a new understanding for Stacey. It wasn't a matter of Jennifer having less desire or fewer orgasms. Jennifer's desire, eroticism, and orgasm pattern was unique to her.

The couple therapist was a wise clinician who realized that sexuality has a 15–20% role. Couple sexuality energized their bond and allowed each to feel desire and desirable. Sexuality provided emotional energy to process other relational issues to ensure their bond would be satisfying and secure.

Jennifer and Stacey married as soon as it became a legal option. As an aging lesbian couple they valued their marriage, including a vital sexual relationship.

Dealing with Hidden Agendas and Manipulation

We have focused on acceptance of sexual differences, including orientation, atypical arousal, and gender fluidity. We have confronted the mistaken assumption that these are pathological. This section does not negate our approach, rather it encourages you to be aware of the cases where sexuality is subverted by hidden agendas or manipulation. This is applicable to all individuals and couples but is especially relevant for those dealing with sexual diversity issues. People take advantage of vulnerable individuals, especially sexual minorities. The most common hidden agenda involves financial scams. This includes money for fake social action organizations, false stories of transgender and gay people in need, manipulation for financial gain, people leading a double life who are being blackmailed. It is demoralizing to realize the extent of negative motivations and hidden agendas which harm sexual minorities. This book and the sexual health field assume positive motivation and advocate individual and couple well-being. This affirming approach is empowering. However, be aware that there are individuals and groups who are manipulative and have hidden agendas.

Exercise: Implementing Healthy Sexuality for Sexual Minorities

There is great diversity in terms of sexual orientation, sexual arousal, and gender expression. This makes creating a personally relevant exercise challenging. What sexual minorities have in common is that your sexual attitudes, behaviors, emotions, and values are special, not mainstream. We suggest that you do this exercise by yourself and then share understandings with your partner, best friend, or counselor.

Be honest in responding to these questions, no politically correct or socially desirable responses accepted.

1. Do you accept your authentic sexual self whether bisexual+, a fetish arousal pattern, gender fluidity, or your unique sexual issue?
2. Are there people (partner, best friend, sibling, minister, counselor) who support your authentic sexual self?
3. Have you incorporated your authentic sexual self into your relationship so you feel desire and desirable? Does sexuality have an integral role in your life and relationship?
4. Are there areas of vulnerability, confusion, or secrecy regarding sexuality which you feel shameful about?

If there are problems in any of these areas, we strongly recommend seeking therapy. You deserve sexuality to be healthy and satisfying in your life.

Turn toward your partner and process answers to these four questions. Are you an intimate sexual team in dealing with these issues? You are not clones of each other. By its nature, atypical sexual expression is experienced differently by each partner. The core issue is whether your partner accepts you and "has your back". Feeling genuinely accepted is crucial. Do not allow manipulation, a contingent sexual self-esteem, or a contingent relationship. This exercise promotes examining and affirming acceptance, pride, and your right to satisfying sexuality.

Summary

Most people who read this chapter are mainstream aging couples. The benefit is greater awareness and acceptance of people who are sexually different than you.

For readers who belong to a sexual minority, the message is self and partner acceptance. It's more than passive acceptance. Embrace your authentic sexual self and affirm that you deserve sexuality to have a positive role in your life and relationship. Gay people are not just first-class, being gay is optimal for you. Many gay, lesbian, bisexual+ people grew up burdened by secrecy and shame. It is your right as an aging adult to celebrate your sexuality. Many people (especially men) led a secret life of a fetish arousal, BDSM, or cross-dressing. You kept your sexual life secret from your spouse. Healthy sexuality confronts shame and promotes acceptance. You could not find your authentic sexual voice in rigid, oppressive gender roles. Gender fluidity gives you the space and freedom to express yourself.

Accepting sexual diversity is not at the expense of mainstream couples and values. It is an acknowledgment of individual, couple, and cultural diversity. Affirm the value of sexual diversity, acceptance, and your right to sexual pleasure.

12

ILLNESS AND DISABILITY: DON'T LET IT CONTROL YOUR SEXUALITY

Illness and disability increase with aging. The good news is there is no illness or disability which stops you from being sexual. Embrace the new normal which involves awareness of psychological, biomedical, relational, and sexual challenges. Illness/disability impacts sexual function but does not negate desire for pleasure-oriented touching. As your sexual response becomes less strong and reliable, psychological, relational, and psychosexual skill factors become more important for your sexual relationship. Biomedical interventions are necessary to deal with medical problems, but these do not promote desire/pleasure/eroticism/satisfaction. Medications or medical remedies aren't a stand-alone intervention to cure sexual problems. Adopt a psychobiosocial approach to understanding and managing your illness/disability (McCarthy & Wald, 2017). Accept medical problems, do not deny or avoid. However, do not give them control over your sexual relationship. You are more than your illness/disability. Dealing with illnesses like cancer or heart disease and disabilities such as impaired eyesight or living in a wheelchair is your new normal. However, your life is more than the cancer and more than vision problems. Over a period of months people accept their medical condition and learn to adapt. Rather than looking back to the time before the illness, accept it is part of your life. Acceptance is the basis of well-being. Approach your illness/disability from the perspective of what can be changed, what can be modified, and what needs to be accepted and worked around.

Sexuality is a crucial component in dealing with illness/disability. Maintain intimacy, quality of life, and sexuality. Affirm the vitality of your life and relationship. Sexuality is a rebellious act—you affirm pleasure and vitality. Desire/pleasure/eroticism/satisfaction continue to be a valued part of your relationship. Affirm your right to pleasure. You own your body; the illness/disability does not own it.

A heart condition, including side-effects of medications, can cause fatigue and muscle pain which interferes with sexual response. In this situation, touching is usually for comfort rather than sexual arousal. You cannot expect your body to be sexually responsive when drained. Your body deserves the comfort of touching as well as its capacity to experience pleasure and arousal.

Even though your sight is impaired, your other senses are available to compensate, especially sense of touch. Your body is adaptable—take advantage of your body's strengths and adaptability. Do not allow your body to be defined by the disability/illness.

Be aware of two unhealthy extremes. The common extreme is feeling your sexuality is defined and controlled by the illness/disability. Sexually, you are more than your illness. The other extreme is denial—feeling you are super sexual and ignoring the reality constraints of your illness/disability. Acceptance of the medical reality is the basis for embracing the new normal. Accept that you have cerebral palsy, cancer, impaired hearing, or diabetes. You neither deny nor do you define yourself by the medical problem. Meet physical challenges and commit to individual and couple sexuality. Often, your spouse is also dealing with medical challenges. Sexuality and illness is not a zero-sum game. Enlist your spouse as your intimate friend in approaching physical realities. When both partners value a satisfying sexual relationship you have a solid foundation for sexuality and aging. Accept the illness/disability and unite to maintain desire/pleasure/eroticism/satisfaction.

Each illness and disability has unique challenges. Commit to not letting medical problems control you. Breast cancer or prostate cancer is approached as the joint enemy. Recognize the impact it has on your sexuality. Sexuality is even more of a team effort when dealing with a disease/disability (Bober & Falk, 2020). When one spouse has cancer, the ill person has more of a burden than the healthy spouse. Yet, cancer is a challenge for you as a couple. Dealing with the cancer is the prime agenda. In addition, quality of life, including intimacy and sexuality, is a couple challenge. For example, the man with prostate cancer deals with the new normal of orgasm without ejaculation through his penis (the ejaculate goes to the bladder). His acceptance is facilitated by her sexual flexibility. Openness to sexuality after prostate cancer is crucial for both partners. Engage in exploration to determine what is right for your sexual healing journey. Although it is healthy to mourn losses caused by the cancer and its treatment, it is not healthy to obsess or engage in "if-only" thinking.

This approach of acceptance and exploration is equally true when dealing with breast (or other gynecological) cancers. Cancer does not make you less of a sexual woman. The new normal entails changes in sexual function, but desire for intimacy, pleasuring, and eroticism remains. It is especially important to turn toward your spouse as your intimate and erotic ally. Accept your new body and its capacity for pleasure.

Aspects of Illness and Disability

In the medical field the emphasis, as it should be, is on assessment and treatment of the illness. Whether the primary care physician, specialist, nurse, physical therapist, or rehabilitation specialist, their training is on biomedical dimensions. You want to be a knowledgeable patient who understands your body and your illness. Be active in the healing process. Develop a relationship with the medical professional where you ask questions and trust the information and suggestions.

Emily remembers her mother who dealt with a multitude of chronic health problems and surgeries. The mother had to undergo a complex orthopedic surgery. The internist asked whether she wanted to work with the best surgeon (who had an extremely poor bedside manner) or a surgeon who was empathic and supportive. She chose the best surgeon.

You need a competent physician. Ideally, the physician, nurse practitioner, and/or physician's assistant is willing and able to discuss psychological, relational, and sexual issues regarding the illness/disability. However, don't expect the ideal. Who on your medical team is the most helpful in discussing psychological and sexual issues? If the answer is no one, seek a consultation with an individual, couple, or sex therapist. This might be a single consultation, an ongoing therapeutic resource, or someone to consult on an as-needed basis. The psychologist or rehabilitation counselor is empathic and a good listener. Use all your resources to deal with the illness/disability and enhance the quality of your life. Most mental health clinicians see individual clients. If you deal with issues as a couple be sure the clinician is competent in providing a couple consultation.

Whether the illness is diabetes, heart disease, asthma, cancer, multiple sclerosis, or disabilities such as inability to walk unassisted, hearing problems, or being in a wheelchair, the issue is quality of life, including touching and sexuality. Rather than emphasize losses caused by the disability, focus on the challenge of maintaining desire/pleasure/eroticism/satisfaction with your disability. Psychologically, do you accept the new normal? Each medical problem has its own challenges and coping techniques, but the basic challenge is similar. How to ensure that touch and sexuality continues to have a 15–20% role for you individually and as a couple. Don't fall into the trap of allowing your life to be controlled by the illness/disability and giving up sexuality. Do not go to the other extreme of pretending that the illness/disability does not impact your psychological, relational, and sexual health. The new normal involves awareness of the limitations and challenges of your disability/illness without allowing it to control your life and sexuality.

Dorthey and Clifford

Throughout their 52 years of marriage Dorthey (80) and Clifford (83) had encountered a number of physical, psychological, and relational problems while maintaining a satisfying relationship. They had a good quality of life in their 80s. They helped friends and relatives deal with serious illnesses, some resulting in death, commonly the death of the husband.

They had a three-year age difference. Dorthey worried about Clifford's health even more than her own. Neither was facing life-threatening illness, but each was dealing with chronic medical problems. Fourteen years ago Clifford survived a heart attack and nine years ago Dorthey was treated for skin cancer. Both were taking multiple medications. Dorthey took a low dose anti-depressant medication to facilitate sleep. In addition, she took medications for arthritis and high blood pressure. Clifford was taking blood pressure medication, cholesterol medication, as well as two medications for diabetes. Their illnesses and medications were monitored by the gerontologist both used as their primary care doctor. Each consulted with the physician four times a year. Multiple illnesses and medications are the norm for men and women in their 80s. Dorthey felt her health was good while Clifford listed his health as fair, although he felt healthier than most 83-year-old men.

For the last two years, Dorthey and Clifford resided in an independent living community where they had easy access to cooking, cleaning, and health promotion activities. Clifford had resisted moving to the facility, but Dorthey and their adult children had lobbied to make this change before a medical crisis forced them to. In retrospect, Clifford agreed it was a wise move at the right time.

A major challenge was to enjoy variable, flexible couple sexuality featuring sensual or erotic scenarios when sex did not flow to intercourse. This is a common challenge, especially for couples in their 70s and 80s. Like most couples, intercourse was the center of their sexual lives for 50 years. Like most women, Dorthey could be orgasmic during intercourse as well as with erotic sexuality either before or after intercourse. Sex always ended in intercourse until their mid-50s. Dorthey and Clifford were proud that they were able to make the transition from totally predictable intercourse to Good Enough Sex (GES). Intercourse was highly valued, but when sex did not flow to intercourse they enjoyed either a sensual or erotic scenario. Clifford was grateful that Dorthey was his intimate and erotic ally in making this transition. Clifford knew men who either gave up sex because the "machinery didn't work", became dependent on a pill or injection which eventually let them down, or went to a massage parlor for paid sex. Clifford turned to Dorthey and together they learned to enjoy flexible sexuality which included intercourse but wasn't dependent on intercourse. This promoted vital and satisfying sexuality in their 50s, 60s, and 70s. However, now in their 80s and dealing with a number of medical problems and medication side-effects they, especially Clifford, were feeling sexually stressed.

They scheduled a joint consultation with their gerontologist. She was a good listener and open to discussing sexual problems. However, she was not a sex expert. The physician could recommend a sex therapist, but neither was interested at that time. She assured them that sex was a common problem and their concerns were normal. She congratulated them on the caring and security of their marriage and maintaining a sexual relationship. The physician made it clear that it was normal to stop sex at 80, but did not advise that. She emphasized intimacy and touching generally, but without a specific sex focus. This was helpful but missed the issue that Clifford needed to process—the role of intercourse. Clifford had used pro-erection medications for the past ten years, eventually settling on Cialis an hour before a sexual encounter. In his early 70s, Clifford found that 80% of sexual experiences flowed to intercourse. In his later 70s this declined to 40%. What was particularly helpful was when Dorthey used a vaginal lubricant and guided intromission. However, at 83 Clifford's comfort and confidence with erections and intercourse had dissipated. Clifford felt he needed more in terms of a biomedical intervention. The doctor said that in her clinical experience some men found penile injections promoted reliable erections. The other intervention that many men found helpful was the external penile pump. Clifford had been an engineer, so the penile pump appealed more than an injection. Dorthey was open to trying whatever Clifford preferred. If he wanted to try the injection, he would need to be the one doing the injection—it would feel anti-erotic for her. Typically, couples try an intervention two or three times to see if it is the right fit for them. They decided to utilize the pump and placed a band on the base of the penis so the erection would last 20–30 minutes. Clifford was optimistic. They engaged in pleasuring before introducing the pump. Dorthey felt subjective arousal of 7 and Clifford felt 5, but believed the pump would heighten his arousal because he had a usable erection. Unfortunately, the opposite occurred. Clifford became very self-conscious. Self-consciousness is anti-erotic. His subjective arousal was −5. Dorthey was willing to try again, but Clifford felt turned-off and was no longer interested in the pump. Dorthey called the physician to inquire about other medical intervention. The physician recommended consulting a couple sex therapist who specialized in therapy with aging couples. It is never too late to seek couple sex therapy.

Years before, during treatment for Dorthey's cancer, she consulted a psychologist who was a specialist in coping with cancer. Clifford had attended two therapy sessions.

The sex therapist used the four-session assessment model with the first session as a couple to reinforce that sexuality and aging is a couple issue. The clinician congratulated them on their marital, sexual, and health successes, and asked the crucial question about personally relevant goals. She reinforced Clifford and Dorthey's commitment to maintaining physical health and a satisfying marriage. She was not surprised to learn that they had not spoken directly about sexual goals. The clinician supported what the gerontologist said about intimacy and touching. In addition, they needed to establish specific sexual goals, including the role of intercourse.

In their individual psychological/relational/sexual history sessions she urged each spouse to be blunt and forthcoming. She saw Clifford first and found he was much more sexually demoralized than Dorthey realized. Clifford was feeling sexually hopeless and was reluctant to share this with Dorthey. He strongly disliked the pump, did not want to try injections, and had lost faith in pro-erection medications. Fear of intercourse failure dominated his sexuality. He believed he was a sexual disappointment to Dorthey and that she felt sorry for him. A very bleak and demoralizing view of himself and sexuality.

The contrast with Dorthey's approach was dramatic. She appreciated the gerontologist's listening and support, but felt the sexual recommendations were not helpful. She wanted a pro-sexual approach. Specifically, she wanted the therapist to support their bond as a first-class sexual couple who could enjoy erotic sexuality, especially manual stimulation to orgasm. This validation would allow them to stop intercourse. Dorthey likened stopping intercourse to their decision to stop oral sex eight years ago. Dorthey enjoyed receiving more than giving oral sex. She did fellatio because Clifford found it erotic. However, after

Clifford developed breathing problems, giving oral sex was no longer positive (or even possible) for him. Dropping oral sexuality from their repertoire was easy to accept because manual stimulation was pleasurable and erotic for both. They had good memories of vital, satisfying oral sexuality, but it was not a good fit now. Dorthey said that this was true of intercourse. Neither she nor Clifford enjoyed intercourse now, even when it was functional. The time for intercourse had come and gone. Sexuality which focused on intimacy, pleasuring, and manual stimulation to orgasm was the right approach for them now. Dorthey was easily aroused and orgasmic with manual stimulation and enjoyed giving manual stimulation. Clifford's erotic response was a turn-on for her. Dorthey expressed her ambivalence. She did not enjoy Clifford's ejaculation in her hand—she found that "yucky". She had not shared this with him. Was it acceptable to have him finish stimulation to orgasm or was that selfish? Clifford wanted Dorthey to enjoy couple sexuality. When she raised this problem, he accepted a change in sexual technique.

Dorthey valued intimacy and pleasure but wanted more from marital sexuality. She wanted eroticism, orgasm, and vitality. She did not want sexuality removed from her life. She wanted to share eroticism with Clifford. Dorthey had enjoyed intercourse but giving it up at 80 was not a major loss. She worried that Clifford could not accept the cessation of intercourse.

In listening to Clifford, the clinician was aware of an ambivalence that was not there with Dorthey. When they gave up oral sex Clifford was relieved because it was no longer comfortable or pleasurable. This was also now true of intercourse. However, throughout life Clifford had associated masculinity with intercourse. It felt like he was giving up the core of sex. Clifford was aware how much easier it was to be aroused and orgasmic with manual stimulation, but felt it was less "manly". Clifford had accepted GES because intercourse was still part of their relationship. Giving up intercourse felt like he was letting Dorthey down—it was a "bridge too far". The therapist didn't lecture Clifford but did make it clear that Dorthey could accept the loss of intercourse and that they needed to mourn the loss together. The therapist promised to further clarify this in the couple feedback session.

She carefully reviewed Clifford's reaction to the medical interventions. Clifford found these a sexual turn-off. He had no desire to utilize them nor did Dorthey. Clifford was worried that Dorthey could not accept a sexual life without intercourse. The therapist facilitated an exploration of the role and meaning of intercourse in the past and now.

The therapist asked Clifford his preferences and feelings about sexuality at 83, specifically regarding intercourse. Clifford took a deep breath and said he really enjoyed giving and receiving manual stimulation. He did not want to stop intercourse forever but, unless there was a new biomedical intervention, he could accept the loss of intercourse as long as Dorthey could.

The 90-minute couple feedback session was the most honest Clifford and Dorthey had been about sexuality in 52 years. For Dorthey, mutual manual stimulation ending with Clifford's self-stimulation to orgasm was her preferred way to share sexuality. Clifford was surprised by her bluntness. It allowed him to embrace couple sexuality (hopefully for as long as they lived). They acknowledged the loss of intercourse, including joking about their best intercourse experiences, especially on their first wedding anniversary.

They agreed to a yearly follow-up session to ensure couple sexuality continued to be pleasurable and satisfying. This increased motivation and accountability. If there were changes in physical health which impacted sexual health or if there were sexual concerns, they would schedule a "booster session". Dorthey and Clifford reported to the gerontologist that couple sex therapy had been extremely helpful.

Consultation with a Medical Specialist

Medical specialists are experts at the assessment and treatment of specific illnesses/disabilities. They undergo advanced training to master their specialty whether cardiology, endocrinology, urology, gynecology, psychiatry, gerontology, neurology, or pain management. They focus on their specialty rather than general medicine. It is unlikely they received specific training in sexual health. You are asking the specialist to step outside their comfort and knowledge zone and consult about sexuality and aging. You are more likely to get their attention and help if you attend as a couple and are clear this will be a single consultation (perhaps with a follow-up). What can the specialist contribute to biomedical components of your sexual relationship? Typically, the prime contribution is increasing understanding of how your illness/disability impacts sexual function and dysfunction. What are the vascular, neurological, and hormonal changes involved in your illness/disability? Can these be changed, modified, or do you need to accept and work around the problems?

The most common intervention involves medications. Are these helpful and at what dosage should you use them? Sometimes the specialist suggests a different medication with fewer sexual side-effects. Sometimes the suggestion is a different time to take the medication. Are there changes in behavioral health habits which can improve your sexual health? Examples involve improved sleep behavior or reducing alcohol consumption before a sexual encounter.

Physicians want to cure problems, but in most illnesses/disabilities with aging the issue is medical management. Not expecting a "miracle cure" makes it easier for the specialist to talk about managing your illness to diminish its impact on sexual health.

Another suggestion is to consult a sexual medicine specialist. This could be a psychiatrist, gynecologist, urologist, or endocrinologist with specific training in sexual function and dysfunction. Sexual medicine specialists emphasize biomedical interventions, as well as attending to psychological and relational issues.

Exercise: Creating and Implementing a Plan to Deal with Illness/Disability

This exercise asks you to utilize and implement the psychobiosocial approach to illness/disability. It has both an individual and couple component. Remember the core guideline—you are not looking for a cure, but to enhance couple sexuality. Use all your resources to promote sexual health as you cope with your illness/disability.

Do you accept your illness/disability? Are you a good patient? Are you open to promoting desire/pleasure/eroticism/satisfaction in the context of your illness/disability? Are you committed to not allowing the illness/disability to control your sexuality?

List the physical challenges of your illness/disability. Be specific about which are changeable, which modifiable, and which need to be accepted and worked around.

Share your list with your spouse and discuss their perceptions and feelings. How does the illness/disability impact couple sexuality? This is not an analytic/objective science approach. It is a personal, emotional exploration of the roles and meanings of sexuality in your lives as an aging couple. Accept the illness/disability and be open to dealing with the new normal. Address challenges as an intimate sexual team. What do you need to do psychologically, medically, and relationally to promote couple sexuality? What have you learned from your past which promotes sexuality at this time in your life? List at least two and up to five interventions to try. Be sure that at least one involves a biomedical resource. As well, make sure at least one is a psychological or relational resource.

The concept of sexuality as a team sport is particularly important when faced with illness/disability. Rather than wishing you (or your partner) did not have a medical problem, turn toward your partner with the understanding that this is a couple challenge. Accept the new normal and use all of your psychological, biomedical, and relational resources to reinforce couple sexuality in the context of the illness/disability.

Chronic Medical Conditions

Many illnesses and disabilities will improve with treatment. Unfortunately, some medical problems become chronic and severe over time. Examples include multiple sclerosis, poorly controlled diabetes, and cancer which has metastasized. Denial is psychologically and sexually unhealthy. Giving up sex is unhealthy. When medical problems are chronic and worsening it is important to use all your resources and approach sexuality as a couple challenge. There is not a perfect resolution, but there are positive sexual alternatives.

In the situation where the spouse is transferred to palliative care and dealing with the dying process, touch is necessary whether affectionate, sensual, playful, or erotic touch. This affirms your right to be a sexual person until you die. One of the hardest things about the Covid 19 virus was that people had to die alone. Having a loved one there to hold your hand facilitates dying with comfort and dignity.

Maintain pleasure-oriented touch when dealing with chronic, deteriorating medical problems. Turn toward your partner and share your body. At this point sex is usually asynchronous, but healthy for both partners. Maintain a genuine connection. Touch is a statement that you are an intimate team whose lives are more than the chronic illness.

Summary

When dealing with a disability/illness (whether acute or chronic) sexuality issues are ignored by health care professionals. Don't allow that to happen. You deserve to engage in touching and experience pleasure. Accept the new normal and value desire/pleasure/eroticism/satisfaction. You are more than your illness/disability. Individually and as a couple use all your psychological, biomedical, and relational resources to promote intimacy, pleasuring, and eroticism. If your primary care physician or specialist is not comfortable or able to answer your questions, consult a sex counselor, therapist, or sexual medicine specialist. Value your sexual relationship as you navigate life with the illness/disability. Sexuality can still have a 15–20% role in your life.

13

SEXUALITY FOR SINGLES: ENJOYING YOUR SEXUAL SELF

There are many single people after age 60. This can be a result of the death of a spouse, a divorce, because they never married, or a relationship ended. Aging women and men deserve sexuality to have a positive role in your life whether in a relationship or not. This includes the freedom of masturbation, a sexual friendship, or a lover relationship. Some people have casual sex, "hook-up" sex, or (especially men), paid or on-line sex.

People do not choose to be single with aging, but if that's the reality be aware of options which can promote your psychological and sexual well-being. Also, be aware of options which could subvert your well-being. Stay away from those traps.

These are many more single women than men in your 60s, 70s, and 80s. However, the stereotypes of sexually active single men are not true, nor is it true that single women do not have sexual options.

The theme of this chapter is expressing sexuality so it has a positive role in your life. Of course, one option is to be non-sexual. We do not view this as a healthy choice for the majority of women and men. Remember, the essence of sexuality is giving and receiving pleasure-oriented touch. This contributes to quality of life with aging whether you are single or in a relationship.

Being single after 60 confronts these stigmatized issues—being single, aging, and sexuality. You have the right to be sexual—you deserve sexual pleasure. For many, the ideal resolution is to remarry and have a satisfying, secure, and sexual marriage. If that is a viable option, we encourage you to pursue it, but realize you are in a lucky minority. Marrying for "socially desirable" reasons is high risk—it makes you vulnerable to people with manipulative or hidden agendas. The loneliest people are not single, they are caught in an alienated or destructive marriage. You don't need marriage to justify being sexual.

Accepting Being Single

Acceptance is the basis of your well-being generally as well as sexually. Being single is nothing to be ashamed of or embarrassed about. It is more socially acceptable to be a widow or widower, especially if you had a satisfying marriage. We all have regrets about psychological and sexual aspects of our past, but that does not negate the good memories and feelings about our lives. Perhaps the best parting gift is the dying spouse acknowledging the value of your marriage and saying that you deserve happiness in the future, including a second marriage and satisfying sexuality. This does not negate your first marriage; it honors the legacy of that marriage. A second marriage which is satisfying, secure, and sexual is the ideal, but is not the only good option. In fact, marriage is an option for only a minority of single people. Unhealthy second (or third) marriages subvert psychological and sexual well-being.

A common option is a lover or sexual friend relationship. A lover relationship is longer, exclusive, and has a greater role in your life. This includes introducing the lover to your extended family, including adult children and grandchildren.

A sexual friendship is valuable, but by its nature you realize it will eventually end. Don't change your life for a sexual friendship. The sexual friend might be a work colleague, neighbor, someone from a dance group, out of town friend. You meet twice a week, twice a month, or twice a year. You treat each other with empathy and kindness and share sexual experiences. Seldom do you include the sexual friend in family activities. The sexual friendship might last six weeks, six months, or six years. It is not a lifetime commitment. Hopefully, the sexual friendship ends well, but often there is disappointment or conflict. A year later you look back at the sexual friendship with positive feelings.

Whether a sexual friendship, lover relationship, life partnership, or second marriage, relational sexuality is welcomed and adds to the quality of your life.

Sex is not the most important factor in a healthy relationship. Sexuality is a shared pleasure which energizes your relationship. Don't stay in a bad relationship because of sex. The sexual paradox is that conflictual, dysfunctional, or avoidant sexuality can destroy a good relationship, but good sex cannot save a bad relationship.

Non-Relational Sexuality

Traditionally, the culture has made negative moral judgments about non-relational sexuality. This includes casual (acquaintance), "hook-up", anonymous, on-line, or paid sex. Rather than accept the stereotypes and judgments, carefully examine your situation and values. Is sex in a non-relational context healthy for you? Traditionally, judgments were much harsher for women than men. Shaming the person is of no value for anyone.

Casual sexual encounters are about opportunity. As long as the sexual experience is consensual, not manipulative, and not based on a hidden agenda it is acceptable. A key to casual sex is managing expectations. Don't expect more from the sex than it can offer. People have a casual sexual relationship for one month or one year, but don't expect it to turn into a serious relationship. Take it for what it is—an opportunity to share pleasure and orgasm. Don't give it an emotional significance it doesn't deserve.

Hook-up sex, which may or may not involve intercourse, is sex focused. It is often fueled by alcohol and impulsivity. Most of the time the hook-up is a one-time event although people hook-up with the same partner on an intermittent basis.

Anonymous sex involves no personal intimacy and is usually driven by loneliness or alcohol. We do not recommend anonymous sex, but as an adult you have a right to your psychological and sexual choices. Be aware of manipulative or hidden agendas, don't let sex destabilize your life.

On-line sex has a number of variations, commonly involving trading sexual pictures or erotic stories. On-line sex often involves self-stimulation to orgasm.

Paid sex, especially for men, has existed throughout time and cultures. The most common types are massage parlors and prostitutes. In addition to previous caveats, be aware of manipulation—especially financial. Barry had clients who spent thousands of dollars on prostitutes, massage parlors, strip bars, or sex websites. The man was caught in an out-of-control sex behavior pattern.

With non-relational sex it is particularly important to utilize safer sex which means using condoms (male or female condoms) and having a yearly HIV test and STI screen.

The Value of Masturbation

The majority of aging adults—partnered or single—occasionally masturbate. This is true for both females and males (Laumann et al., 1994). The positive motivations for masturbation include feeling sexual but no available partner, to stay in touch with your body and its capacity for pleasure, to explore erotic fantasies and scenarios, as a tension reducer, to promote sleep, and to celebrate sexuality. Of course, people masturbate for negative motivations—a compulsive pattern, isolation, anger, boredom. You need to address these issues because in these cases masturbation reinforces a self-defeating pattern.

Masturbation is not only normal; it is physically and psychologically healthy for both women and men. It keeps you in touch with your body, especially your capacity for pleasure and orgasmic response. In the same way it is healthy to have regular exercise, masturbation is healthy for sexual expression. You don't want genital response to atrophy or to become sexually self-conscious. Whether or not you are involved with partner sex, masturbation is a symbol of your right to pleasure.

The Value of Relational Sexuality

Whether relational sex involves a potential life partner (marriage), a lover relationship, or a sexual friendship, partner sex adds value to your life. You need the partner as your sexual friend more than you did 20 years ago. The mantra of desire/pleasure/eroticism/satisfaction is particularly relevant for couple sexuality in your 60s, 70s, and 80s. The core dimension is desire—openness, positive anticipation, deserving pleasure. Be open to giving and receiving pleasurable touch, do not feel pressure to perform. Accept the multiple roles, meanings, and outcomes of couple sexuality. Sharing your body and sexuality feels more vulnerable with aging yet is more genuine. Sex is more than a foreplay, intercourse, orgasm routine. Healthy sexuality is based on your power to say "no" to sexual scenarios and techniques that are not acceptable. You have confidence your partner will honor your veto. This facilitates sexual openness. Ideally both partners affirm intimacy, pleasuring, and eroticism. Confront individual performance demands, replacing this with a couple pleasure orientation. Ideally, sex involves easy arousal, intercourse, and orgasm. Believing that all sex should be that way sets you up for disappointment. Single people embrace variable, flexible sexual response. The female–male sexual equity model and the Good Enough Sex (GES) model are the basis of healthy sexuality in your 60s, 70s, and 80s.

Special Challenges for Aging Single Women

The prime challenge is to accept your rights as a sexual woman who deserves pleasure. Women generally, and single women specifically, are de-eroticized by the media and culture. What nonsense. You are a sexual woman until you die. Some aging women find arousal and orgasm easier than your partner. Your sexual receptivity and responsivity facilitate his sexual response. Men are distracted by performance anxiety, especially erectile anxiety and fears of intercourse failure. He learns to piggyback his arousal on yours. Accept playful and erotic touch rather than depending on visual stimuli for arousal. You come into your own sexually in your 60s and 70s.

Feel free to implement your sexual scenarios rather than follow his scenario as you have for ten or 50 years. Your sexual socialization did not include female–male sexual equity; introduce it now in your relationship. The most important dimensions are replacing foreplay with pleasuring and replacing passivity with actively giving and receiving touching. Take advantage of aging to express your "sexual voice" without fear of partner or social judgment. Enjoy your authentic sexual self. Barry recalls a 68-year-old twice divorced woman who established a sexual friendship with a 62-year-old widower. He was interested in remarrying because he valued the security of marriage (she believed he wanted a woman to take care of him). She was not interested in a third marriage but was open to a sexual friendship. For her, feeling desire and desirable was an aphrodisiac, reinforcing the value of pleasurable and erotic touching. He learned new sexual scenarios and techniques which he integrated in his second marriage. A year later she was invited to his wedding. The bride thanked her for helping him regain his sexual confidence.

You do not require marriage to justify desire and pleasure. A successful marriage involves much more than good sex. Good sex has value for itself whether in a life partnership, lover relationship, or sexual friendship. A partnered relationship enhances psychological and sexual well-being. When a relationship ends because it is no longer viable, whether due to the man's decision, a change in life circumstances, your decision, or a sad ending, it doesn't mean the relationship was a mistake. Ideally, the relationship ends in a non-destructive manner. The emotion is sadness rather than anger.

A common challenge is dealing with your partner's sexual problems whether erectile dysfunction (ED), ejaculatory inhibition (delayed ejaculation), premature ejaculation, or low desire. In addressing sex dysfunction do not blame yourself or make it your problem. Be his intimate and erotic ally in changing the problem, but don't try to do it for him. A common example is ED. Many men after 60 (perhaps a majority) experience some degree of erectile anxiety or full-blown ED. You did not cause the problem. ED involves a combination of psychological, biomedical, and social/relational factors. Easy, totally predictable erections are the exception not the norm for men after 60. The most common problem, whether he uses Viagra or not, is that as soon as he becomes erect he rushes to intercourse. The healthy strategy is to enter into erotic flow (subjective arousal of 8 or 9) before transitioning to intercourse. If sex does not flow to intercourse you transition to an erotic scenario or a sensual scenario. Although ED can be caused by a lack of attraction or reflect a relational problem, in most cases that is not the cause. Either way, it is not your responsibility to resolve the problem. Approach this as an intimate team. You can accompany him to see a sex therapist and/or a physician. However, do not make resolving the problem a test of you or your sexuality. When you make it your problem you cause further problems for you, him, and the relationship.

Can you feel good about a sexual relationship which includes erotic sexuality, but not intercourse? Most (but not all) women enjoy sensual, playful, and erotic sexuality. Many aging women enjoy erotic sexuality more than intercourse. Most women feel good about both synchronous and asynchronous sexuality, others are fine with being the receiving partner during asynchronous sex, and still others are fine being the giving partner. Remember, sexually one size does not fit all. What is the right fit for you?

Male desire problems are a challenge, especially if he denies the problem or blames you. The most common issues are a sexual secret or a sexual dysfunction (McCarthy & Cohn, 2017). Some women accept a non-sexual relationship and are fine with sex not being part of their lives. Most women miss touching and experience sexual avoidance as distressing. Sexual avoidance could be a sign of a fatally flawed relationship. However, that is not the most likely message. The most common cause is the man's sexual anxiety and embarrassment. Non-married couples benefit from couple sex therapy.

Intimacy, touching, and sexuality contribute 15–20% to the quality of your life. Couples should not stay together because of sex nor should sex be the primary factor in ending a relationship. You deserve sexual pleasure as an aging woman. Don't give a sexual problem more power than it deserves. Don't let fear of being alone cause you to stay in a marginal or destructive relationship. Giving up sex is a loss, but a necessary loss if it is an unhealthy relationship.

You want a relationship where touching and sexuality has a positive role. You don't have to be married or in a life partnership to enjoy sexuality. The flip side is good sex is not worth a bad relationship at 75 (or any age).

Special Issues with Aging Single Men

There are so many myths and misunderstandings about aging single men it is hard to know where to begin. The core guideline is you don't have to prove anything sexually to yourself, your partner, or anyone else.

It is true that aging men are more likely to remarry. It is also true that aging men benefit emotionally and physically from a healthy relationship. What is not true are two extreme beliefs—that aging men have as much sex as they want from a variety of women nor the belief that aging men need a woman and marriage to survive. Don't be influenced by these stereotypes. What is your situation and values? You don't need to prove anything to anyone. What is sexually right for you?

Alternatives include remarrying, developing a lover relationship, being non-sexual, creating a sexual friendship, or engaging in casual sex, hook-up sex, on-line sex, or paid sex.

A challenge is to accept yourself and not give in to stereotypes. Your adult son and daughter lobby you to remarry because they are afraid you cannot take care of yourself. Men function better psychologically and medically when married. You have more chance to remarry whether a woman of your age or younger. Be aware of hidden agendas or women who over promise sex or caretaking. We advise you to be involved at least a year before marrying. Have an honest, blunt dialogue about each person's strengths and vulnerabilities. You cannot ask the woman to be honest unless you are honest with her. Barry's father did not tell his second wife he was diabetic. When dating, he was very social and active. In reality, he was a homebody who was more comfortable with her dog than her. Barry received phone calls from his step-mother complaining how her husband had pulled a "bait and switch". They stayed married for more than 15 years (including nursing him after a massive heart attack and lengthy rehabilitation). She felt it was worthwhile because of family relationships, their home, community connections, grandparenting, and quality of life. However, they should have discussed personal and health vulnerabilities before marrying.

For financial and family reasons some men prefer a lover relationship or sexual friendship. A core issue is to establish and maintain desire/pleasure/eroticism/satisfaction. If you are dealing with ED, ejaculatory inhibition, premature ejaculation, or low desire do you turn toward your partner as your intimate and erotic friend? An advantage of aging is sexual flexibility. You share intimacy, pleasuring, and eroticism. Sexuality with aging is more human and genuine.

Some men choose paid sex as a way to reduce performance pressure. When you go to a massage parlor and pay $50 for a "happy ending" or pay a prostitute you feel it is her responsibility to arouse you. This reduces anxiety and self-consciousness. Be aware that a minority of sex workers have a hidden financial agenda to make you dependent on her. Men are vulnerable to loneliness and manipulation which negates the sexual transaction.

Single men face extreme biases—the pressure of being sexual with a range of women on one extreme and the lonely, pathetic single man on the other extreme. Establish a healthy sexuality which fits your reality and values. Marriage or a life partnership is a wonderful option as long as it is a genuine relationship where you feel loved for who you really are (with strengths and vulnerabilities). You love and accept your partner for who she is.

For some men a sexual friendship is more acceptable. You have a relationship while maintaining your independence and lifestyle. What is the right fit for you? You deserve sexuality to have a positive role in your life.

Caroline

Caroline has a vibrant and satisfying life. She became a widow six years ago when her second husband died of a heart attack. Caroline valued him and their marriage, although it certainly was not perfect. She enjoys her two adult sons and four grandchildren from the first marriage but has minimal contact with her first husband. Caroline keeps distance with her second husband's two adult children. Caroline continues to work 20 hours a week because she enjoys interactions with customers and staff at the local bookstore.

Since becoming a widow she has had three sexual relationships. The first was a sexual friendship with an old friend who lived in an adjacent state and had a marginal marriage. Caroline enjoyed the intrigue and sexual exploration in this new relationship. They met for a weekend at a golf resort. Caroline enjoyed the sense of sexual adventure. She was upset that he was married, but since it was a marginal marriage she did not feel she was undermining it. Caroline realized this was a sexual friendship which would eventually end. Its ending was precipitated by his health crisis. She wished him well but had no interest in the caretaking role.

The second relationship was the most involving, but also the most painful. The man was younger, 51, and interested in marriage. Their relationship had an intense four-month limerence phase which included a week trip to London and several weeks where he stayed at her house. They were compatible and he was interested in her life, including wanting to meet her children and grandchildren (which Caroline decided against). She met his two adult children, one of whom she particularly liked. Of her three partners their sexual relationship was the most vital, although Caroline disliked that he went to sleep immediately after he ejaculated. Caroline was usually orgasmic before him, but not cuddling after sex was disappointing. All men and all relationships have vulnerabilities, but he admitted to none. Caroline learned that he'd been in bankruptcy twice. His finances were problematic at present. He overpromised and overspent. As this came to light Caroline was surprised that her sexual desire increased. Practically, she was put off, but sexually was turned-on. This emotional and sexual roller coaster continued for two more months with dramatic fights and dramatic sex. Caroline felt more like a teenager than an aging woman. She was convinced that things would right themselves, but the objective part of her realized this was a better sexual relationship than a life partnership. She went out of her way to shield her children and grandchildren from this part of her life, although her daughter-in-law was concerned about the relational drama.

The crisis that ended that relationship was his arrest for a DUI. This was objective feedback—he was not a healthy man nor was this a healthy relationship. It took two weeks for him to give back the keys to her house. Caroline was surprised that through all the turmoil sex continued to be vital. Her sexual socialization was that intimacy and warm feelings were the base for sexual desire. Her desire and response were not motivated by intimacy and certainly not warm feelings. In fact, by the end she was appalled by his behavior.

The sexual friendship Caroline is now involved in is with a twice divorced 66-year-old man she met through mutual friends. She is hopeful this will be a continuing relationship. They share a number of activities including playing bridge and golfing. Caroline told friends they did not have great sex, but it was pleasurable. He took Viagra and over 85% of encounters led to intercourse. When he wasn't erect enough for intercourse, he would stimulate her to orgasm and then she would stimulate him to orgasm. This was more of a functional sexual transaction than a vital couple sexuality. Caroline felt they could do better, but he believed he was doing as well as he could given his age. They were together sexually two or three times a month. Caroline would masturbate when she felt "horny" but was pleased she was in a sexual friendship. Caroline enjoyed "beating the odds" as a single woman and remaining sexual after 65. Rather than comparing sex with other partners Caroline accepted this relationship for what it was.

An unexpected plus for Caroline was being a sex educator for her granddaughters and grandson. She took a pro-sex stance and advocated for female–male sexual equity. Her grandchildren enjoyed hearing her perspective on cultural changes in sexual roles and expectations.

Making Wise Psychological, Relational, and Sexual Decisions

You have the ability to make "wise" (good emotionally and practically, short and long term) decisions as an aging single adult. You deserve sexual pleasure in your life until the day you die. You want partner sex to have a positive role, not a dramatic, destabilizing role. Whether a second marriage, life partnership, lover relationship, or sexual friendship, touching and sexuality energize your life. You are no longer controlled by oppressive social norms or "emotional choices" which result in destructive relationships. You want sexuality to fit the reality of your life and life options.

For some people, the decision to stop being sexual is the right one, but not for the majority. You don't need marriage or a perfect relationship to justify being sexual. You feel desire and desirable, not controlled by unrealistic love or sex performance images.

An advantage of aging is that you recognize the range of roles, meanings, and outcomes of sexuality. The romantic love/passionate sex/idealization model is replaced by a positive, realistic approach to desire/pleasure/eroticism/satisfaction. You are a proud aging adult in an adult sexual relationship. Pleasure-oriented couple sexuality has replaced individual perfect performance sex. Make wise decisions about the role of sexuality in your life.

Exercise: Your Sexual Options as a Single Person

This exercise asks you to carefully review sexual options as a single woman or man over 60 and to make a wise decision. Be honest with yourself, do not give "socially desirable" answers. You can process past sexual experiences, but your power to make wise decisions is in the present. Answer these questions honestly:

1. Personally and relationally when was sex healthiest in your life?
2. Personally and relationally when was sex problematic?
3. Do you feel you deserve sexuality to have a positive role in your aging process?
4. How do you feel about masturbation—do you deserve to enjoy masturbation?
5. How do you feel about a sexual friendship—the most common form of partnered sex with aging?
6. Would you be comfortable with a lover relationship?
7. Are you open to remarriage or a life partnership?
8. How do you feel about casual, hook-up, cybersex, or paid sex?
9. What do you need to be aware of so sexuality does not have a negative impact on your life?

Share your responses with a best friend, counselor, or minister for their perspective and feedback. Be sure this is someone who is helpful, not judgmental. Remember, it's your life and only you know if it's a wise decision.

Summary

Being single does not stop you from enjoying your body, touching, and sexuality. You have a range of options to express sexuality both with masturbation and partnered sex. Set positive, realistic goals for sexuality as a single person.

The most common type of partnered sex is a sexual friendship. You don't need marriage to enjoy sexuality. A healthy second (or third) marriage is ideal for many people but might not be an option for a variety of practical, emotional, financial, and family factors. Being single is much preferable to a marginal or destructive marriage.

An advantage of couple sexuality is that it recognizes variable, flexible sexual expression rather than sex as an individual performance. You can enjoy sensual, playful, and erotic scenarios in addition to or instead of intercourse. You need your partner in a way you didn't 20 years ago. Aging sexuality is more human and genuine, especially when you focus on pleasure-oriented touching.

You are a sexual person until the day you die. You deserve for intimacy, pleasuring, and eroticism to have a role in your life.

14

CELEBRATING SEXUALITY AND AGING

You are a sexual person from the day you are born until the day you die. The core of sexuality is giving and receiving pleasure-oriented touching. You owe it to yourself, your partner, and your relationship to maintain vital, satisfying sexuality with aging. Broad-based couple sexuality includes sensual, playful, and erotic scenarios in addition to intercourse. The Good Enough Sex (GES) model is the foundation for couple sexuality with aging. It promotes psychological and relational well-being.

The sexual paradox is that healthy sexuality has a small, positive (15–20%) role in your relationship, but sex dysfunction, conflict, and especially avoidance has an inordinately powerful negative role. Giving up sex is a very poor choice which impacts both partners and your relationship. Contrary to gender expectations it is the man who chooses to stop sex because he has lost confidence with erections and intercourse. It isn't that he wants to stop, he is frustrated and embarrassed that he can't have "normal sex". He makes the choice unilaterally and conveys it non-verbally. This self-defeating choice is totally unnecessary and has a major negative impact on the woman and your relationship. An advantage of sexuality and aging is it promotes variable, flexible couple sexuality. Sex is not an individual pass–fail performance test. Sexuality is a couple process of giving and receiving pleasure-oriented touching. Sexuality includes sensual, playful, and erotic scenarios in addition to intercourse. Rather than avoidance, turn toward each other as intimate and erotic friends. GES values intercourse, but not as a performance demand. If the sexual encounter does not flow to intercourse, comfortably transition to either an erotic or sensual scenario. There is no reason to panic or apologize, and especially not to avoid.

Mutual, synchronous sex is the ideal. Yet, asynchronous sexuality (positive but better for one partner) is the norm. Asynchronous sexual experiences are healthy. They become more common with aging. A critical dimension of GES is acceptance that 5–15% of sexual experiences are dissatisfying or dysfunctional. This too is a normal aspect of couple sexuality with aging.

Sexuality is important for quality of life because it affirms pleasure as well as feelings of desire and desirability with aging. Individually and relationally, you celebrate sexual vitality and satisfaction. In your younger years sex was driven by novelty, adventure, and exploration. Sexuality with aging is more human and genuine. Couples, especially men, feel proud they have "beaten the odds". All the good things about sexuality come to fruition with aging. You need each other sexually in a way you didn't 20 years earlier. The mantra of desire/pleasure/eroticism/satisfaction becomes more relevant with aging.

"Responsive sexual desire" is key for the majority of women and men. Desire is the core dimension—facilitated by positive anticipation, deserving pleasure, freedom and choice, unpredictable sexual scenarios and techniques. Pleasure, rather than performance, promotes sexuality. Eroticism is important for women as well as men. Integrated eroticism is vastly different than the porn version or illicit images. Eroticism is more than intercourse. Eroticism facilitates vital sexuality for both genders. Satisfaction is the second most important dimension. Although orgasm is highly valued, satisfaction is much more than orgasm. Satisfaction is feeling good about yourself as a sexual person and energized as a sexual couple. Men learn to value variable orgasmic response rather than demanding a single orgasm during intercourse. For many, if not most, aging couples, arousal and orgasm is easier for the woman than the man. You learn to piggy-back your arousal on her arousal. Celebrate your flexible, variable sexual style.

Although mutual, synchronous sexuality remains the ideal, asynchronous sexuality is more common and valued. Nuances regarding roles, meanings, and outcomes of couple sexuality are prominent with aging.

Female–Male Sexual Equity

Most of us grew up with the traditional male–female double standard. The double standard provided clear rules of how to act sexually. The assumption was that sex was the man's domain with love and intimacy the woman's domain. Scientifically, the double standard is almost totally wrong. Hopefully, you broke out of this rigid, oppressive model years ago, but for many remnants of the double standard interfere with your sexuality now. With aging it is clear that the double standard is harmful. Sixty is not too late to adopt the female–male sexual equity model. This allows you to celebrate sexuality as intimate and erotic friends. Sexual expression is more genuine. Sexual similarities between women and men become clearer with aging. Psychologically, relationally, and sexually each spouse is a fully functioning person. The challenge for women is to reinforce your "sexual voice", especially your "erotic voice". The challenge for men is to value intimacy and non-demand pleasuring for yourself and accept broad-based pleasure and erotic expression. GES is the key to male sexuality with aging. Intimate, interactive couple sexuality is much superior to autonomous sex. Intimacy, pleasuring, and eroticism are shared domains, not governed by rigid gender roles. Turn toward each other as sexual allies who share desire/pleasure/eroticism/satisfaction.

Five Dimensions of Touching

Most couples have only two dimensions (gears) of touch—affection and intercourse. Sex is defined by intercourse. In the "intercourse or nothing" approach nothing usually wins. The average American couple have sex (intercourse) a bit more than once a week (59–62 times a year). The average range is 3–12 times a month. A no-sex marriage is being sexual less than once a month and low-sex marriage less than twice a month (McCarthy & McCarthy, 2020).

Don't accept this old model of sex. Our new model features five gears (dimensions) of touch: (1) affection, (2) sensual, (3) playful, (4) erotic, and (5) intercourse. Think of this like a five-gear car. Enjoy the ride; not all touching needs to end in fifth gear.

Affectionate touch is a crucial foundation but is not sexual. Affectionate touch involves holding hands, kissing, and hugging. Affection anchors you with physical attachment. In terms of subjective pleasure/arousal, affectionate touch is a 1 on a 10-point scale.

Sensual touch involves non-genital touching—body massage (excluding genitals), touching when you go to sleep or on awakening, back or foot rubs, cuddling on the couch while watching a DVD. In terms of subjective pleasure/arousal, sensual touch is in the 2–3 range.

Playful touch integrates genital and non-genital touching. This involves whole-body massage, seductive or romantic dancing, playing games like strip poker or Twister, bathing or showering together. Playful touch involves subjective pleasure/arousal in the 4–5 range.

Erotic touch involves manual, oral, or rubbing stimulation. The focus is on high-intensity feelings and sensations in the 6–10 range (10 being orgasm). Erotic sexuality usually transitions to intercourse, but not as a demand or rigid expectation. Many people (especially women) enjoy orgasm with erotic sexuality.

Fifth gear involves intercourse. Rather than thinking of intercourse as a pass–fail individual performance, intercourse is a natural continuation of the pleasuring/eroticism process. Do not move to intercourse as soon as you can (subjective pleasure/arousal 4–5), transition to intercourse when you experience erotic flow (subjective pleasure/arousal 8–9). A key concept is to continue multiple stimulation during intercourse (clitoral stimulation, buttock stimulation, testicle stimulation, kissing, and private erotic fantasies).

There are two key concepts. First, sensual, playful, and erotic scenarios are sexual—it's not intercourse or nothing. Accepting variable, flexible sexuality is crucial with aging. This involves a broad-based understanding that sexuality is much more than intercourse. Second, subjective pleasure/arousal is more important than objective function (erection, lubrication, orgasm). Sharing pleasure is more important than sex performance. Couple sexuality with aging has a range of roles, meanings, and outcomes. This is different than the sex dysfunction model. An example is that even when sex is objectively dysfunctional (lack of erection, non-orgasmic response), it still can be subjectively pleasurable and satisfying.

A crucial concept is the value of asynchronous sexual experiences. The best sex is mutual and synchronous—both partners experience high levels of desire/pleasure/eroticism/satisfaction. Most sexual experiences are asynchronous (positive but better for one partner than the other). With aging, asynchronous sexuality becomes more common. The scenario is a 10 for one while 7 or 3 for the other. There are a variety of asynchronous scenarios which can enhance your relationship with aging. Embrace GES, synchronous and asynchronous scenarios, and broad-based sexuality so you enjoy sexuality in your 60s, 70s, and 80s.

Exercise: Maintaining Vital and Satisfying Sexuality with Aging

You owe it to yourself, your partner, and your relationship to maintain sexual desire and satisfaction with aging. This exercise asks you to create a specific plan to operationalize these good intentions. How can you maintain desire/pleasure/eroticism/satisfaction?

Begin with desire, the most important dimension. The key is "responsive sexual desire" for both partners. What type of touch facilitates desire and how is it integrated in your relationship? What type of affectionate touch are you receptive to? What type of sensual touch feels most inviting? Does playful touch elicit sexual responsiveness? Are your preferences similar to or different than your partner's? In addition, be aware of types of touch or initiations which are turn-offs.

List two to six touching and initiation scenarios which facilitate anticipation and receptivity. In addition to responsive desire what other cues facilitate sexual initiation? Examples include willingness to reconnect, celebrate a special occasion, response to an erotic fantasy, break a morose mood, being sexual after a walk, to affirm love or desirability.

For you, what is the essence of pleasure-oriented touching? Some couples value affectionate touch, others sensual touch while listening to music, others a playful scenario of helping remove her bra while she plays with you as you slip out of your pants. In terms of pleasuring, do you like taking turns or is your preference mutual pleasuring? Is pleasuring best nude in bed or sitting clothed in front of the fireplace? Is "making out" pleasurable now (or was it better in the past)? Does it help to have a prohibition on intercourse or are you comfortable with a go with the flow approach? Share your preferred pleasuring strategies and techniques.

What are your favorite erotic scenarios and techniques? Focus on the present, not what was erotic in the past. Do you prefer partner interaction arousal, self-entrancement arousal, or role enactment arousal? Eroticism as an aging couple is an act of rebellion against societal norms. Eroticism portrayed on the internet is anti-intimacy and anti-aging. You owe it to yourself and your marriage to integrate eroticism into your sexual relationship. Create at least one synchronous erotic scenario and two (one for each) asynchronous scenarios. Integrated eroticism is integral to couple sexuality with aging. Eroticism usually flows to intercourse, yet eroticism is a valued experience in itself. Intense sensations and emotions are part of your sexual life as an aging couple.

Create sexual scenarios which are satisfying for you personally and relationally. Be aware that satisfaction is more than orgasm. Unlike in your younger years, male orgasmic response becomes variable. You may orgasm during intercourse, with manual, oral, or rubbing stimulation, or not be orgasmic during that encounter. Working to reach orgasm is self-defeating. When you eventually achieve orgasm it feels more like a relief than a satisfying experience.

An advantage of aging for both women and men is following your feelings rather than a rigid sex script. Savor experiences where both are orgasmic and satisfied. Be aware of experiences where physically you orgasmed, but psychologically did not feel satisfied. A particularly important awareness is when you felt emotionally satisfied even though you were not orgasmic. Remember, satisfaction is more important than orgasm. It is an example that subjective pleasure is more important than objective function. For you, what is the most important factor in satisfaction? Is that true for your spouse? Do you feel satisfied with asynchronous sexual experiences? Can you feel satisfied with non-orgasmic experiences?

In completing this exercise, be clear what you value about couple sexuality with aging. Do you accept variable, flexible, broad-based sexuality? Is sharing pleasure really more important than sex performance? Are you an intimate sexual team who celebrate desire/pleasure/eroticism/satisfaction?

Accepting Your Sexual Past and Celebrating Your Sexual Future

A major challenge is the ability to process your past in an accepting manner. Processing past learnings involves willingness to "own" positive and negative psychological, relational, and sexual experiences. Avoid two extreme traps—denial on one extreme and despair on the other. We do not know anyone, including ourselves, who have not experienced regret or sadness about past experiences. It is part of being a human being—you make mistakes and bad choices. Rather than pretending or denying, accept and process painful and even destructive experiences. You need to own your behavior in order to learn from the past.

Defining yourself or sexuality by the mistakes of the past leads to despair. Owning bad choices allows you to move on rather than remain stuck. The core guideline is to learn from the past, but not let your sexuality be controlled by the past. Your power for change is in the present.

Barry spent 42 years as a therapist and was struck by the number of clients who were unwilling to genuinely process their past so they could be a fully functioning person and couple in the present. Processing does not mean reliving the past, it means owning your previous choices and experiences. Regret is healthy, shame is destructive. Shame gives control and power to the past. An example is a relationship which ended in a destructive manner. You usually begin as a limerence couple and end as a sad couple. It is destructive to hurt/harm the partner and remain stuck in the blame/anger cycle. This controls your life and burdens your present relationship. The majority of divorces are "bad"—the primary emotion is anger. In processing negative experiences, it is not helpful to demonize the ex-spouse. What is helpful is accepting the divorce and recognizing your learnings about yourself and relationships. Don't put yourself on a pedestal and blame the ex-spouse for everything. Take responsibility for your behavior, including negative sexual experiences. Own these learnings so you don't repeat them in your present relationship. Process positive and negative learnings from the previous relationship. Be a better person and create a satisfying, secure, and sexual second marriage. Rather than demonizing the ex-spouse learn from the power struggle so in this marriage you approach issues such as desire discrepancies as an intimate sexual team. Treat desire as a couple issue rather than pressuring your spouse or retreating to avoidance. It is easy to take the simplistic, blaming approach rather than being honest and owning your relational and sexual learnings.

The core message is to live your life in a healthy manner. Affirm desire/ pleasure/eroticism/satisfaction. You can't make up for the past, but you can live in the present so that sexuality has a 15–20% role. Take pride in your life and relationship.

Lila and Ferguson

Lila, 75, and Ferguson, 77, have been married 51 years. This is Lila's first marriage and Ferguson's second. They do not have a perfect life or marriage but are proud of their lives and relationship. Sex was frequent in the first two years of the marriage, but best in their 50s during the "couple again" phase. As an aging couple they are pleased with their broad-based GES relationship.

Ferguson values their two adult children and four grandchildren. He is saddened that he has no relationship with the daughter from the first marriage (the marriage broke up two months after she was born and the ex-wife moved to California and allowed no contact). In retrospect, Ferguson married the wrong woman because of the unplanned pregnancy. Lila and Ferguson were married three years before their planned, wanted son was born.

Lila feels that they lost each other during the parenting years. Sex was a source of conflict rather than bringing them together. She loved

Ferguson, but often did not like him, especially around sex issues. Ferguson was a traditional man who approached sex as intercourse with a focus on frequency. He saw himself as sexually liberated and blamed Lila for being easily sexually distracted. Once involved, Lila was orgasmic during intercourse. If not, she was usually orgasmic during afterplay. In retrospect, Lila regretted not having serious conversations about sexuality. Instead, their conversations were about parenting, work, money, and household chores. Ferguson agrees they should have broken down traditional gender barriers and created an equitable sexual relationship in which both valued intimacy, pleasuring, and eroticism. Instead, Ferguson built resentment and felt sexually rejected. Underneath the anger he worried about not being masculine enough or attractive enough. Had she fallen out of love with him? He would sulk when his sexual initiation was rebuffed. He worried she would have an affair or fall in love with another man. Male friends, especially when drinking, would talk incessantly about women having affairs. Lila felt that kind of talk was demeaning. She was acutely aware of sexism and men one-upping each other talking about sex. She was put off, but didn't raise these issues with Ferguson.

As often happens it took a crisis to challenge the status quo. Although men deny this, a common crisis is your first "sensitizing" sexual experience (not having an erection sufficient for intercourse). This occurred at age 49 for Ferguson. Lila and Ferguson often had sex on Saturday night after two drinks while watching an R-rated video. For the first time, Ferguson lost his erection. Although Lila orally stimulated him, he could not maintain an erection strong enough for intercourse. She assured him that it was okay, there were times she had not been aroused. However, this violated Ferguson's assumption that he should be able to have intercourse anytime Lila was willing. He didn't say anything but felt devastated. The next evening Ferguson masturbated and was relieved that "the machinery worked".

After a sensitizing experience, few men return to totally predictable erection and autonomous sex. Rather than being afraid and viewing this as a devastating loss, Ferguson approached erection and sexuality in a healthy manner. His challenge was to be an aware lover. The sensitizing experience opened Ferguson to responsive sexual desire and intimate, interactive sexuality. This was congruent with Lila's sexual experience. Ferguson turned toward Lila as his sexual friend to share desire and satisfaction. GES was his opportunity to embrace a new approach to sexuality. Ferguson was a wise man who understood the value of broad-based male and couple sexuality. He looks back on this transition and credits Lila with encouraging him to meet this sexual challenge. Lila enjoyed couple sex now more than in their first two years. This was powerfully reinforcing for Ferguson. Although not an overnight change, over the next four months Ferguson turned toward Lila as his intimate and erotic ally. Lila welcomed his openness, especially responsive sexual desire. They were so used to Ferguson's spontaneous erections that it was a challenge to accept his desire and erection coming from sensual and playful touching. Realizing that he needs her help to build pleasure and eroticism was a turn-on for Lila. Ferguson now has "grown-up" erections rather than "show-up" erections. They took advantage of their new couple sexual style and the couple again phase to enjoy vital, satisfying sexuality. Lila especially felt validated as a sexual woman in her 50s rather than feeling she had to catch up with Ferguson. This approach to intimacy, pleasuring, and eroticism won him over. It was a better fit than the model of male predictability and control. They truly were an equitable sexual team.

Now in their 70s, Lila and Ferguson welcome a new phase in couple sexuality. Lila's sexual receptivity and responsivity is vital for Ferguson's sexual response. He needs her in a way he didn't 20 years before. They increasingly utilize self-entrancement arousal scenarios. Ferguson and Lila enjoy mutual, synchronous intercourse while accepting asynchronous and flexible sexuality.

A meaningful ritual is being sexual at each celebratory event—their anniversary, each other's birthday, Christmas, Easter, July 4, Valentine's Day, Labor Day, and Thanksgiving. Celebratory sex is a great strategy.

Ferguson and Lila are committed to being a sexual couple until the day they die. Ferguson emphasizes "beating the odds" while Lila emphasizes physical attachment and affirmation as a loving couple.

Positive, Realistic Sexual Expectations

Throughout this book we have emphasized GES, especially positive, realistic sexual expectations. This is particularly important in your 60s, 70s, and 80s. The keys to satisfaction are acceptance and positive expectations. This changes with aging—important factors are illness and disability, especially the side-effects of medications to treat the medical problems. Unfortunately, most physicians and nurses are not comfortable or skilled at providing sexual information and counseling. If you consult the medical provider as a couple, you will receive more help. Do not accept the traditional approach of being told you are too old or too ill to worry about sex. You have a right to intimacy, pleasure, and sexuality. The issue is how best to express your sexuality. Adopt the definition of sexuality to include sensual, playful, and erotic scenarios in addition to intercourse. You can enjoy sexuality which does not involve intercourse. Desire, pleasure, and satisfaction are the important factors. The individual sex performance model must be dropped.

Pleasure and subjective arousal are better measures than intercourse frequency. Affectionate, sensual, and playful touch is more important than orgasm. Value an intimate and erotic bond which energizes your relationship. The two traps are avoidance on one extreme and demanding sex performance on the other. A key strategy is positive, realistic expectations for sharing pleasure with a range of roles, meanings, and outcomes. This includes welcoming both synchronous and asynchronous sexual experiences.

Summary

We have co-authored 16 books on relationships and sexuality. This is our favorite book. At ages 77 and 75 with 54 years of marriage, our message is to value a broad-based couple sexuality. Our goal is to motivate and empower you to enjoy sexuality with aging.

Redefine sexuality as a couple process of sharing pleasure. Sexuality involves sensual, playful, and erotic scenarios in addition to intercourse. Adopt the female–male sexual equity model to replace the traditional double standard. Embrace GES and drop the individual sex performance model. The joy of sexuality with aging is that it's genuine and human. You need each other as intimate and erotic friends. This is true whether the sex was marvelous or problematic. Utilize all your psychological, biomedical, and relational resources to enhance your sexuality. Take pride in beating the odds. Enjoy yourself, your partner, and your relationship throughout the aging process.

Appendix A

CHOOSING A SEX, COUPLE, OR INDIVIDUAL THERAPIST

This is a self-help book, not a do-it-yourself therapy book. Many older individuals and couples are reluctant to consult a therapist, feeling that to do so is a sign of weakness, a confession of inadequacy, or an admission that your life and relationship are in dire straits. This is even truer for men who are fearful that the therapist will blame them for couple and sex problems. In reality, seeking professional help means that you are a wise person and couple who realize there is a problem. You have made a commitment to address the problems and promote individual, couple, and sexual health.

The mental health field can be confusing. Sex therapy and couple therapy are clinical subspecialties. They are offered by several professionals: psychologists, marriage therapists, pastoral counselors, psychiatrists, social workers, and licensed professional counselors. The professional background of the clinician is less important than her competence in dealing with sexual, couple, and individual problems.

Many people have Medicare or other health insurance that provides coverage for mental health; thus, they can afford a private practice therapist. Those who have neither insurance nor financial resources can consider a university or medical school mental health clinic, a family services center, or a local mental health clinic. Most clinics have a sliding fee scale program.

When choosing a therapist, be direct in asking about credentials and areas of expertise. Ask the clinician what would be the focus of therapy, how long therapy is expected to last, and whether the emphasis is specifically on sexual problems or on individual, communication, or relational issues. Be especially diligent in asking about university degrees and licensing. There are poorly qualified individuals—and some outright quacks—in any field.

One of the best ways to obtain a referral is to call or search on-line for a professional organization such as state psychological association, marriage and family therapy association, or a mental health organization. You can obtain a referral from a family physician, minister, imam, rabbi, or a trusted friend. If you live close to a university or medical school, call to find what specialized psychological or sexual health services are available.

For a sex therapy referral, contact the American Association of Sex Educators, Counselors, and Therapists at aasect.org. Another resource is the Society for Sex Therapy and Research at sstarnet.org.

For a couple therapist, check the website for the American Association for Marriage and Family Therapy at therapistlocator.net.

If you want to consult a psychologist for individual or couple therapy for anxiety, depression, behavioral health, and other problems check the Registry of Health Service Providers in Psychology at findapsychologist.org.

Feel free to speak by phone with two or three therapists before deciding who to see. Be aware of your level of comfort and degree of rapport with the therapist as well as whether the clinician's assessment of the problem and approach to treatment is right for you. Once you begin, give therapy a chance to be helpful. There are few miracle cures. Change requires commitment; it is a gradual and often challenging process. Although many people benefit from short-term therapy (fewer than ten sessions), most find the therapeutic process requires four months or longer. The role of the therapist is that of consultant rather than decision-maker. Therapy requires effort, both during the session and between sessions. Therapy helps you change attitudes, behaviors, and emotional reactions. It takes courage to seek therapy. Therapy can be a tremendous help in assessing and changing sexual, couple, and individual problems. Therapy allows you to be a healthier aging person and couple.

Appendix B

SUGGESTED READINGS

Bethell, K. (2020). *An essential guide to aging well.* New York: Routledge.

Butler, R. & Lewis, M. (2002). *The new love and sex after 60* (2nd ed.). New York: Ballantine.

Foley, S. (2005). *Sex and love for grown-ups.* New York: Sterling.

McCarthy, B. (2014). *Therapy with men after 60.* New York: Routledge.

Metz, M. & McCarthy, B. (2004). *Coping with erectile dysfunction.* Oakland, CA: New Harbinger.

Price, J. (2005). *Straight talk about sex after 60.* New York: Seal.

Price, J. (2011). *Naked at our age.* New York: Seal.

REFERENCES

Althof, S. (2006). Sex therapy in the age of pharmacotherapy. *Annual Review of Sex Research*, 17, 116–132.

Anderson, K. (2017). Sexual affectional orientation and diversity. In C. Pukall (Ed.), *Human sexuality* (2nd ed., pp. 259–283). Ontario, Canada: Oxford.

Basson, R. (2007). Sexual desire/arousal disorders in women. In S. Leiblum (Ed.), *Principles and practice of sex therapy* (4th ed., pp. 25–53). New York: Guilford.

Bergeron, S., Rosen, N., Pukall, C., & Corsini-Munt, S. (2020). Genital pain in women and men. In K. Hall & Y. Binik (Eds.), *Principles and practice of sex therapy* (6th ed., pp. 180–201). New York: Guilford.

Bethell, K. (2020). *An essential guide to aging well*. New York: Routledge.

Bober, S. & Falk, S. (2020). Sexuality and cancer. In K. Hall & Y. Binik (Eds.), *Principles and practice of sex therapy* (6th ed., pp. 455–469). New York: Guilford.

Brotto, L. & Velten, J. (2020). Sexual interest/arousal disorder in women. In K. Hall & Y. Binik (Eds.), *Principles and practice of sex therapy* (6th ed., pp. 13–40). New York: Guilford.

Brotto, L., Yule, M., & Gorzalka, B. (2015). Asexuality. *Journal of Sexual Medicine*, 12, 646–660.

Frank, E., Anderson, C., & Rubinstein, D. (1978). Frequency of sexual dysfunction in "normal" couples. *New England Journal of Medicine*, 229, 111–115.

Ghazzani, A. (2020). *Healthy aging: Well-being and sexuality at menopause and beyond*. Coral Gables, FL: WSB Publisher.

Gottman, J. & Silver, N. (2015). *The seven principles for making marriage work*. (2nd ed.) New York: Harmony.

Graham, C. (2014). Orgasm disorders in women. In Y. Binik & K. Hall (Eds.), *Principles and practice of sex therapy* (5th ed., pp. 89–111). New York: Guilford.

Hyde, J. (2005). The gender similarities hypothesis. *American Psychologist*, 60, 581–592.

Johnson, S. (2008). *Hold me tight*. Boston, MA: Little-Brown.

Kalogeropoulos, D. & Larouche, J. (2020). An integrative biopsychosocial approach to the conceptualization and treatment of erectile disorder. In K. Hall & Y. Binik (Eds.), *Principles and practice of sex therapy* (6th ed., pp. 87–106). New York: Guilford.

Laumann, E., Gagnon, J., Michael, R., & Michaels, S. (1994). *The social organization of sexuality: Sexual practices in the United States*. Chicago, IL: University of Chicago.

Lindau, S., Schumm, L., Laumann, E., Levinson, N., O'Muircheartaign, C., & Waite, L. (2007). A study of sexuality and health with older adults in the United States. *New England Journal of Medicine*, 357, 762–774.

Maltz, W. (2012). *The sexual healing journey* (3rd ed.). New York: Willian Morrow.

McCarthy, B. & Cohn, D. (2017). Treatment of male hypoactive sexual desire disorder. In W. Ishak (Ed.). *The textbook of clinical sexual medicine*, pp. 133–153. New York: Springer.

McCarthy, B. & McCarthy, E. (2012). *Sexual awareness* (5th ed.). New York: Routledge.

McCarthy, B. & McCarthy, E. (2018). *Finding your sexual voice*. New York: Routledge.

McCarthy, B. & McCarthy, E. (2019). *Enhancing couple sexuality*. New York: Routledge.

McCarthy, B. & McCarthy, E. (2020). *Rekindling desire* (3rd ed.). New York: Routledge.

McCarthy, B. & McCarthy, E. (2021). *Contemporary Male Sexuality*. New York: Routledge.

McCarthy, B. & Metz, M. (2008). The Good Enough Sex model: A case illustration. *Sexual and Relationship Therapy*, 23, 227–239.

McCarthy, B. & Oppliger, T. (2019). Treatment of desire discrepancy: One clinician's approach. *Journal of Sex and Marital Therapy*, 45, 585–593.

McCarthy, B. & Ross, L. (2017). Integrating sexual concepts and interventions into couple therapy. In J. Fitzgerald (Ed.), *Foundations for couple therapy* (pp. 355–364). New York: Routledge.

McCarthy, B. & Wald, L. (2013). New strategies for assessing, treating, and relapse prevention of extramarital affairs. *Journal of Sex and Marital Therapy*, 39, 493–509.

McCarthy, B. & Wald, L. (2017). Psychobiosocial approach to sex therapy. In Z. Peterson (Ed.), *The Wiley-Blackwell handbook of sex therapy* (pp. 190–201). Hoboken, NJ: Wiley-Blackwell.

McKinlay, J. & Feldman, H. (1994). Age related variation in sexual activity and interest in normal men: Results from the Massachusetts male sexuality study. In A. Rossi (Ed.). *Sexuality across the lifespan* (pp. 261–285). Chicago, IL: University of Chicago.

Metz, M., Epstein, N., & McCarthy, B. (2017). *Cognitive-behavioral therapy for sexual dysfunction*. New York: Routledge.

Metz, M. & McCarthy, B. (2004). *Coping with erectile dysfunction*. Oakland, CA: New Harbinger.

Metz, M. & McCarthy, B. (2007). The "Good Enough Sex" model for couple sexual satisfaction. *Sexual and Relationship Therapy*, 22, 357–362.

Metz, M. & McCarthy, B. (2012). The Good Enough Sex (GES) model: Perspective and clinical applications. In P. Kleinplatz (Ed.), *New directions in sex therapy* (2nd ed., pp. 213–230). New York: Routledge.

Mintz, L. & Guitelman, J. (2020). Orgasm problems in women. In K. Hall & Y. Binik (Eds.), *Principles and practice of sex therapy* (6th ed., pp. 109–133). New York: Guilford.

Mosher, D. (1980). Three psychological dimensions of depth involvement in human sexual response. *Journal of Sex Research*, 16, 1–42.

Perelman, M. (2009). The sexual tipping point. *Journal of Sexual Medicine*, 6, 629–632.

Price, J. (2011). *Naked at our age*. New York: Seal Press.

Weiner, L. & Avery-Clark, C. (2017). *Sensate focus in sex therapy*. New York: Routledge.